The ITALIAN SLOW COOKER

The ITALIAN SLOW COOKER

Michele Scicolone

PHOTOGRAPHS BY ALAN RICHARDSON

HOUGHTON MIFFLIN HARCOURT
BOSTON   NEW YORK   2010

www.hmhbooks.com

Library of Congress Cataloging-in-Publication Data
Scicolone, Michele.
  The Italian slow cooker / Michele Scicolone ;
photographs by Alan Richardson.
     p. cm.
  Includes index.
  ISBN 978-0-547-00303-0
  1. Electric cookery, Slow. 2. Cookery, Italian. I. Title.
  TX827.S36 2010
  641.5'884—dc22
                              2009013744

Printed in the United States of America
Book design by Kris Tobiassen
Food styling by Anne Disrude
Prop styling by Betty Alfenito

DOC 10 9 8 7 6 5 4 3

Acknowledgments

Many friends and acquaintances gave me advice, suggestions, opinions, cooking tips, recipe ideas, and, most of all, the encouragement I needed to write this book. *Mille grazie*, a thousand thanks, to all of them, especially Susan Wyler, who was the first to tell me how popular slow cookers are today. The Rival Company and All-Clad were most helpful with information and supplied me with the latest equipment.

Rux Martin, my editor, shared her enthusiasm for slow cooking and guided me with her insightful suggestions. Thanks to everyone at Houghton Mifflin Harcourt and the supporting cast who contributed to this book, including Anne Chalmers, Teresa Elsey, Sara Shaffer, and Jacinta Monniere.

Photographer Alan Richardson's photos capture the warmth and deliciousness of slow-cooked food. It was a pleasure working with him, Anne Disrude, and Betty Alfenito. All three know Italian food so well, and their love and appreciation of it comes through in the beautiful photos. I'm grateful to designer Kris Tobiassen for her inviting design. Thanks to my agent, Judith Weber, of Sobel Weber Associates, for her friendship and for helping me to focus my ideas.

Thank you, too, to Charles, my husband, who is the ultimate taste tester. I can always rely on him for his honest opinion and a good wine to match.

Contents

Introduction

Near the neighborhood where I often stay in Rome is a Tuscan restaurant with a small window in its façade. A large, round, greenish glass bottle sits in a small brick alcove perched above a wood-fired stove. Every morning, a cook fills the *fiasco*, as the bottle is called, with dried beans, water, and seasonings. All day long, the beans simmer slowly, absorbing the flavors of the garlic and herbs as they swell, becoming tender and creamy. Passing by one day, I salivated at the sight, and I thought, "This is the original slow cooker!" Until that moment, it had never occurred to me to use an electric slow cooker for Italian cooking, but suddenly, there it was.

Not only is a slow cooker perfect for cooking beans, but it's ideal for simmering a Bolognese-style meat ragu, a thick, hearty vegetable soup, or a rich beef stew of the kind I enjoyed in Tuscany. Soups, stews, and pasta sauces, as I had expected, are naturals—no worries about scorching or planning for hours in the kitchen. Just walk away!

With dishes that need lots of babying, the slow cooker really comes into its own, offering advantages the stovetop can't match. Prepared conventionally, polenta is tedious, demanding vigilant stirring so that the cornmeal doesn't scorch. In the slow cooker, it's practically effortless, creamy, and lump-free. The slow cooker makes such a good facsimile of risotto that most of my guests can't tell the difference between it and one made on the stovetop. The texture is a bit softer—slow cooker risotto has plenty of creamy sauce around the rice grains—and since it doesn't require much attention as it cooks, I can serve it on the side even if my main dish is something fussy.

Foods I had never imagined making in a slow cooker turn out beautifully: salmon, halibut steaks, and the Italian-style omelets known as frittatas all emerge in about an hour perfectly moist, allowing me just enough time to set the table or make a salad and a vegetable. Flourless chocolate cakes, puddings, dense cakes with fruits and nuts, and poached fruits are foolproof. The moist, gentle heat is particularly kind to cheesecakes, which never crack as oven-baked versions often do.

Before I got my first model, I had occasionally heard complaints that slow-cooker food was bland or that it all tasted the same. One friend even told me she had given up and put her cooker in the garage, where it was gathering dust. When I asked her to describe why she didn't like it, I was surprised to hear that the recipes she had tried included packaged ingredients and raw meat tossed into the cooker with no preparation. It was easy to understand why she was unhappy. Food that comes out of the pot can only be as good as the ingredients that go into it! Bottled sauces, canned soups, and seasoning packets can make anything taste boring.

I decided to create my own recipes with fresh ingredients distinctively seasoned. Fresh foods not only taste better but are healthier and cost less than packaged products.

Although it's tempting to just toss ingredients into the cooker and take off, browning the meats or sautéing the onions and garlic before slow cooking often means the difference between delicious and dull. Stews, sauces, and braises have deeper, richer flavor and better color, and browning gives the cooking a jump start. Is it essential? No, but these little steps add big flavor and can improve the texture, so they are worth taking to get the best results. For that reason, many manufacturers today make slow cookers with removable liners that can be used directly on the stovetop, so no extra pan is needed. As a bonus, these flameproof crocks are good for reheating food on top of the stove as well.

Like the bottle in that Roman restaurant, the slow cooker doesn't heat up the kitchen, even on the hottest days; it is energy efficient and costs very little to operate; it turns inexpensive cuts of meat succulent and flavorful; and it can feed a crowd. Best of all, I can cook whenever it suits my schedule—on weekends, during the day while I'm out, or when I'm sleeping—knowing that when I finally lift the lid, the result will be unparalleled.

About Slow Cookers

Buying a new slow cooker? Lucky you! Newer models have sophisticated features your grandma never imagined.

If I could design the perfect slow cooker, it would have every one of the features listed below. So far, though, I have not found one model that has all of them.

I CONSIDER SOME ESSENTIAL, SUCH AS:

» High, low, and warm temperature settings.

» A removable insert.

» A signal light so that you can see at a glance when the cooker is operating.

» A timer, preferably one that is digital and easy to read. It helps if there is a beeper that signals when the cooking time is over.

» Flexible programming so that you can set it on high for a time, then have the temperature switch automatically to low.

» An automatic setting that keeps the food warm after the cooking period is over.

THE FOLLOWING FEATURES ARE NICE,
BUT NOT REALLY ESSENTIAL:

» A clear glass lid so that you can peek in without lifting the cover.

» A flameproof insert so that foods can be browned directly on the stove.

» A metal insert—it is not breakable, nor is it as heavy or clumsy as the crockery kind.

» An insert with handles that stay cool.

» An insert with a nonstick surface.

» An oval shape to accommodate roasts and whole chickens.

» Rubber feet so that the pot does not slide on smooth surfaces.

» A retractable power cord.

Techniques and Tips

The recipes in this book are intended for use in a large slow cooker with a 5- to 7-quart capacity, which is ideal for 4 to 8 servings or for quantity cooking with freezable leftovers. A large-capacity cooker also enables you to cook cakes, puddings, and molded foods in pans or baking dishes placed within the insert and can accommodate large cuts of meat and whole chickens.

TIMING in a slow cooker is, in most cases, not very precise. Some foods, especially soups, sturdy cuts of meat, and most sauces, can handle extra cooking time, while delicate foods, such as seafood, eggs, boneless chicken breasts, and cakes, require attention because they can overcook. When you first use your cooker, stick around and observe how it cooks so that you can adjust the cooking time.

FOLLOW THE TEMPERATURE INSTRUCTIONS given in the recipes. Some foods (such as soups, meat, and beans) cook better on low, while others (egg dishes, cakes) fare better on high. Low temperature in a slow cooker is 180° to 200°F, while high temperature is 250° to 300°F (depending on the wattage of the cooker and the temperature and quantity of the food). Note that many older slow cookers cook at a lower temperature. But to ensure food safety, models made in the last ten years or so cook hotter. If you have an older model, plan on a little extra cooking time.

PRECOOK FLAVORING VEGETABLES, like onions, carrots, and celery, on the stovetop or in the microwave, if you prefer, to soften them and draw out their flavor.

POTATOES, CARROTS, AND OTHER ROOT VEGETABLES should be cut into evenly sized pieces so that they all cook through at the same time. When cooking meats and vegetables together, place firm vegetables in the base of the pot and meats on top. This helps the vegetables to cook evenly.

FOR DRIED BEANS, you'll get the best results by soaking them overnight before cooking. The cooking time will vary according to the variety of beans and how fresh they are.

BROWNING MEAT BEFORE SLOW COOKING enhances the flavor, texture, and color. To brown, first pat the meat dry with paper towels. Heat some oil or other fat in a wide pan over medium heat. Place the pieces of meat, such as chops or chunks for stew, in the pan in a single layer so that they don't touch one another. If there is too much meat in the pan, the moisture in the meat will create steam and it will not brown properly. Cook the meat on one side for about 5 minutes. Use tongs to turn the pieces without piercing them. Cook until nicely browned on all sides. Transfer the browned pieces to a plate and continue browning any remaining meat.

FOR FISH AND SHELLFISH, choose thick, sturdy fish steaks and fillets like salmon and halibut and avoid thin, delicate varieties like sole and flounder, which will fall apart. Watch them carefully so that they don't overcook. Add shellfish to a soup or stew toward the end of the cooking time.

FOR CHICKEN, remove and discard any large pieces of fat before cooking and set aside the neck and gizzards for broth. Leaving the skin on a whole chicken helps to keep it intact, but since the skin does not brown, I generally remove it while carving the chicken. When cooking chicken parts, remove the skin from the pieces of dark meat, since it is naturally moist. Leave the skin on white meat, since it's delicate and dries out easily and the skin gives it a little protection. If it looks unappetizing, you can always remove it before serving.

INEXPENSIVE CUTS OF MEAT from the shoulder, rump, and leg turn out especially well in the slow cooker, because their fat and connective tissue melt in the long cooking, moistening the meat and making it tender. Bones add flavor, so choose bone-in cuts when possible. Trim meats to eliminate excess fat.

AVOID UNNECESSARY PEEKING. Lifting the lid and stirring the contents reduces the temperature inside the cooker and may affect the cooking time. It's OK to stir the food once or twice, but avoid opening the cooker, especially in the first hour or two, when the food is coming up to cooking temperature.

YOU MAY NEED TO THICKEN SOUPS AND STEWS, since slow cookers keep in the steam that would normally escape from an open pot. There are several ways to thicken them. The easiest is to simply turn the temperature to high and uncover the cooker for the last half hour or so to allow some of the liquid to evaporate. A quicker way is to pour some of the liquid into a saucepan and boil it on the stovetop until reduced. Another method is to stir together until smooth 1 tablespoon cornstarch or all-purpose flour and 2 tablespoons cool water for every cup of liquid you want to thicken. Blend it into the simmering liquid. Cook for several minutes until thickened slightly.

POLENTA will stay soft and smooth after it's cooked for an hour or more with the cooker set on warm. If it gets too thick, you can loosen it by whisking in a little water, broth, or milk.

WATCH RISOTTO CAREFULLY to make sure the rice does not overcook and become pasty. Risotto does not keep well on warm, so serve it as soon as it is done.

FOR CAKES COOKED IN PANS that will be placed inside the slow cooker insert, you will need a 7-inch springform pan and a 6-cup-capacity baking dish. They are available at many cookware stores and online. But before you buy one, make sure that it will fit the dimensions of your slow cooker.

Slow Cooker Safety

SLOW COOKERS ARE SAFE. Since a slow cooker uses only about as much electricity as a 75-watt light bulb, you can leave it on while you sleep or are out. To be extra careful, keep the space around the cooker clear when it is in use.

TO PREVENT THE GROWTH OF HARMFUL BACTERIA, foods placed in a slow cooker should reach a safe cooking temperature (at least 145°F) as soon as possible. Thaw frozen foods in the refrigerator before adding them to a slow cooker. Don't add oversized pieces of meat to the cooker or cook without the cover, as this may result in temperatures that are not safe.

NEVER HEAT AN EMPTY SLOW COOKER, since it can overheat, cracking the insert or causing damage to the heating element. To preheat the slow cooker before adding hot food, fill it with hot water and set it on high.

DO NOT USE THE SLOW COOKER TO REHEAT COLD FOODS. It takes cold food too long to heat through, which can give harmful bacteria a chance to grow. You can reheat food on the stovetop and then place it in the slow cooker to keep warm.

DON'T UNDERFILL OR OVERLOAD YOUR SLOW COOKER. Since the heating elements are located around the sides of the cooker, it should be filled at least halfway and not more than three-quarters full for even cooking and food safety.

IN THE EVENT OF A POWER OUTAGE WHILE YOU ARE AWAY, throw out the food even if it looks done. If an outage should occur while you are at home, transfer the food to a gas stovetop or an outdoor grill to finish cooking.

DON'T RUN THE SLOW COOKER on an extension cord. The electric cord on a slow cooker is purposely made short to avoid accidents. Find a place to plug it in that is close to an electric outlet.

The Italian Pantry

A well-stocked pantry makes cooking easier. Most of the ingredients used in this book are available in many large supermarkets. Others can be found in Italian specialty markets.

BROTH

Homemade broth is easy to make in the slow cooker, but I always keep canned or boxed broth on hand for emergencies.

BURRATA

This tender fresh cheese from southern Italy is made by shaping fresh mozzarella into a pocket and stuffing it with cream and shreds of mozzarella cheese. It does not have a long shelf life, so be sure that it is fresh when you buy it. If burrata is not available, substitute another soft cheese, like goat cheese or robiola, which is a mild, soft, and creamy cheese from northern Italy that's made from a blend of cow's and goat's milk.

CAPERS

Capers are the flower buds of a bush that grows wild all over the Mediterranean. After they are gathered, they are preserved in salt or vinegar. The salted capers have more flavor, but either can be used. Soak them in warm water for a few minutes to eliminate excess salt or vinegar. Drain and dry the capers before using them.

FARRO

Farro is an ancient variety of grain that is similar in taste and appearance to wheat. (It is sometimes sold as emmer.) Cooks in Tuscany and Umbria, in central Italy, use it often for soups and salads. If you can't find it, substitute spelt, wheat, or barley.

GARLIC

Fresh garlic adds good flavor to many Italian dishes. If you like a mild garlic flavor, use less or add it toward the end of the cooking time.

HERBS

I like to use fresh herbs when they are available, but for convenience, I always have dried on hand. Two herbs that I never use in dried form, however, are basil and parsley, because their flavor is completely unlike that of fresh. When fresh parsley or basil is not available, I leave it out of the recipe or substitute another herb.

Frozen chopped fresh herbs are becoming more widely available and are very handy. I also freeze my own. They darken when they thaw, and although they may not be attractive for garnishing foods, they do add good flavor.

Powerfully flavored herbs like rosemary become stronger during long cooking, so start with a moderate amount. Taste food at the end of the cooking time. If the flavor of the herb has dulled, you can always add a pinch or two more.

MARSALA

Marsala is a fortified wine from Sicily. It has a rich, nutty flavor and is often used in Italian cooking in desserts and in savory dishes such as veal or chicken Marsala. If you can't find it, substitute sherry, port, or a red table wine.

OLIVES

The richness of olives is essential to many Italian dishes. Italian and Greek olives have the most flavor. If they seem too salty or vinegary, soak them in warm water briefly before using. Add the olives at the end of the cooking time so that they retain their bright flavor.

PANCETTA

Pancetta is Italian bacon made from fresh pork belly that is salted and cured and rolled into a cylinder. Generally, pancetta is not smoked. Chopped pancetta adds a meaty flavor to soups and stews. When purchasing pancetta, it's useful to buy it sliced rather than in a chunk. I buy it in quantity, then separate the slices into 2-ounce portions and wrap each one in foil. Stored in an airtight plastic bag, the individual packages keep well in the freezer and thaw quickly. When I need a few ounces for soup or beans, I remove a portion or two from the freezer and let them thaw briefly. While the pancetta is still partially frozen, I chop it into small dice. Some companies sell pancetta already diced in small packages, which is convenient, if you can find it. You can substitute salt pork, bacon, or ham if pancetta is not available.

PARMIGIANO-REGGIANO

Parmesan cheese from Italy should be called by its real name, Parmigiano-Reggiano. To be sure you are buying the genuine article, check the rind to see if the name is stamped into it. Its distinctive flavor is nutty, rich, and tangy all at once. When sprinkled on pasta, soup, or a salad, it livens up the flavor. I buy Parmigiano-Reggiano by the chunk and keep it in the refrigerator both for snacking and for seasoning. The cheese should look moist and fresh, with no sign of molding or drying. If it has been precut, check the expiration date on the package to be sure it is still fresh. At home, wrap it in wax paper and keep it in a sealed plastic bag in the refrigerator.

PECORINO ROMANO

Made from sheep's milk, Pecorino Romano is sharper and saltier than Parmigiano-Reggiano. In many parts of central and southern Italy, Pecorino is used for grating on soups and pasta, especially those made with olive oil instead of butter. I like Pecorino best on tomato sauces and vegetable dishes where I want a more pronounced cheese flavor. Pecorino Romano should be wrapped in wax paper and stored in a sealed plastic bag in the refrigerator.

PINE NUTS

Soft, creamy-textured pine nuts come from the stone pine trees that grow all over Italy. I buy them in bulk at Italian and Middle Eastern stores, where they are much less expensive than the little jars sold in the supermarket. Pine nuts spoil quickly at room temperature, so keep them in the refrigerator or freezer in a tightly sealed container. Substitute slivered almonds or pecans if pine nuts are not available.

DRIED PORCINI MUSHROOMS

Dried porcini mushrooms add concentrated smoky, woodsy flavor to Italian soups and stews. You can generally find them in small cellophane bags at the supermarket. If they are not available, substitute another dried variety. Dried mushrooms should be reconstituted before they are used. Let them soak in warm water to cover for at least 30 minutes. Save the soaking water. If it seems gritty, filter it through cheesecloth or a paper coffee filter. Then add the water and softened mushrooms to the dish.

TOMATO PRODUCTS

Nothing is quite as delicious as a fresh, ripe tomato, but since the growing season is so short, I rely on canned whole tomatoes, sun-dried tomatoes, tomato puree, and tomato paste.

For canned whole tomatoes, try several brands until you find one with tender, sweet tomatoes and no hard, white spots that signify the fruit is unripe. I like the Italian brands best, such as Marinella and La Squisita, because they taste exactly like ripe tomatoes.

Drying intensifies the flavor of tomatoes and preserves them as it eliminates moisture. Dried tomatoes also come marinated in oil and spices, but since those extra flavors are not always desirable, I look for the plain sun-dried tomatoes, which are usually available in the produce aisle.

Tomato puree is good for sauces and other dishes in which you want a smooth, thick texture. Look for a brand that is thick, smooth, and sweet tasting.

For tomato paste, I prefer the kind sold in tubes, because I often need just a tablespoon or two. The paste keeps for months in the refrigerator. Look for tomato paste labeled "double-concentrated" for rich tomato taste. One brand I prefer is Amore.

WINE

Many Italian recipes call for a small amount of wine. For best results, choose an inexpensive dry variety with a neutral flavor. Ask at the wine shop for some suggestions. When you open the bottle, taste the wine. It should be pleasant enough for you to enjoy drinking a glassful. Never cook with a wine that is spoiled or that you don't like, because its flavor will permeate the food and can ruin the dish.

If you prefer not to use wine, substitute broth, juice, or water, as appropriate to the recipe.

Soups

Soups

Butternut Squash Soup

In the fall and winter, I make this smooth, creamy (but creamless) soup all the time. Serve it for lunch with a sandwich or for a light dinner with bread and cheese. It keeps well in the refrigerator for several days.

SERVES 6

- 1 medium onion, chopped
- 2 tablespoons olive oil
- 2 large garlic cloves, chopped
- 1 large butternut squash, about 1½ pounds, peeled, seeded, and cut into 2-inch chunks
- 2 medium potatoes, peeled and cut into 1-inch chunks
- 3 fresh sage leaves or 1 teaspoon dried
- 4 cups Chicken Broth (page 46) or canned chicken broth
  Salt and freshly ground pepper
  Extra-virgin olive oil for drizzling

In a medium skillet, cook the onion in the oil over medium heat, stirring occasionally, until tender but not browned, about 10 minutes. If the onion starts to color, add a tablespoon or two of water and lower the heat slightly. Stir in the garlic and cook for 2 minutes more. Scrape the mixture into the slow cooker. Add the squash, potatoes, sage, and broth. If necessary, add water so that the vegetables are just covered with liquid.

Cover and cook on low for 4 hours, or until the vegetables are soft when pierced with a fork. Let cool slightly, then puree the soup in a blender or food processor. Season with salt and pepper to taste. If the soup is too thick, add a little more broth or water. Serve hot with a drizzle of olive oil.

Clockwise from left:
Butternut Squash Soup (page 19),
Fresh Pea Soup (page 25),
Creamy Cauliflower and Potato Soup (opposite)

Creamy Cauliflower and Potato Soup

A smooth puree of cauliflower, potatoes, and garlic gives the impression of being very rich, when it is, in fact, not at all so.

SERVES 8

- 2 heads cauliflower, about 1¼ pounds each, trimmed and cut into 1-inch pieces
- 2 medium potatoes, peeled and cut into 1-inch chunks
- ¼ cup olive oil
- 4 garlic cloves
- 3 cups Chicken Broth (page 46) or canned chicken broth
- 4 cups water
  Salt and freshly ground pepper
- ½ cup freshly shredded or grated Parmigiano-Reggiano

In a large slow cooker, combine the cauliflower, potatoes, oil, garlic, broth, water, and salt and pepper to taste. Cover and cook on low for 5 to 6 hours, or until the vegetables are very soft.

Let the soup cool slightly, then pour into a blender and puree until smooth. Season to taste with salt and pepper. Reheat gently, if needed. Serve hot, sprinkled with the cheese.

Mushroom Soup with Marsala

Here is an elegant soup for a company or holiday meal. It makes a suitable prelude to roast beef.

SERVES 6 TO 8

- 1 ounce dried porcini mushrooms
- 1 cup hot water
- 2 tablespoons unsalted butter
- 2 large shallots, chopped
- 2 garlic cloves, finely chopped
- 1 pound button mushrooms, thinly sliced
- 4 cups Meat Broth (page 47) or canned beef broth
- 3 cups water
- 2 fresh thyme sprigs or 1/2 teaspoon dried
- 2 tablespoons tomato paste
- 1/2 cup dry Marsala (see page 12) or sherry
- 3/4 cup heavy cream
  Salt and freshly ground pepper
- 1/2 cup freshly grated Parmigiano-Reggiano

Place the dried porcini in a bowl with the hot water. Let stand for 30 minutes. Lift the porcini out of the water and squeeze them to extract more liquid. If the water seems gritty, filter it through a piece of cheesecloth or a paper coffee filter. Set the soaking liquid aside. Chop the porcini.

In a medium skillet, melt the butter over medium heat. Add the shallots and cook, stirring occasionally, until tender and lightly golden, about 10 minutes. Stir in the garlic and cook for 2 minutes more. Scrape the mixture into the slow cooker.

Add the porcini, the soaking liquid, button mushrooms, broth, water, thyme, and tomato paste. Cover and cook on low for 6 to 8 hours, or until the mushrooms are tender. Just before serving, stir in the wine and cream. Add salt and pepper to taste.

Ladle the soup into bowls, sprinkle with the cheese, and serve.

Mushroom-Potato Soup

A chunky soup of mushrooms and potatoes is a specialty of Friuli-Venezia Giulia, in northeastern Italy. For more flavor, use a combination of mushrooms.

SERVES 6

- 1 ounce dried porcini mushrooms
- 1 cup hot water
- 3 tablespoons unsalted butter
- 2 medium onions, chopped
- 1 garlic clove, finely chopped
- 3 medium potatoes, peeled and diced
- 1¼ pounds button or brown mushrooms, such as cremini or portobello (see headnote), sliced
- 5 cups water
- Salt and freshly ground pepper
- ½ cup heavy cream
- 2 tablespoons finely chopped fresh parsley
- ½ cup freshly grated Parmigiano-Reggiano

Place the dried porcini in a bowl with the hot water. Let stand for 30 minutes. Lift the porcini out of the water and squeeze them to extract more liquid. If the water seems gritty, filter it through a piece of cheesecloth or a paper coffee filter. Set the soaking liquid aside. Chop the porcini.

In a medium skillet, melt the butter over medium heat. Add the onions and cook, stirring occasionally, until tender but not browned, about 10 minutes. If the onions start to color, add a tablespoon or two of water and lower the heat slightly. Stir in the garlic and cook for 2 minutes more. Add the porcini and stir well. Scrape the mixture into the slow cooker. Add the potatoes, sliced mushrooms, the soaking liquid, and water. Add salt and pepper to taste. Cover and cook on high for 3 hours or on low for 6 hours, or until the vegetables are tender.

Stir in the cream and parsley. Serve hot, sprinkled with the cheese.

Fresh Pea Soup

Prosciutto gives this soup a rich hammy flavor. Thawed frozen peas work fine in this recipe.

SERVES 6 TO 8

- 1 medium onion, chopped
- 2 tablespoons olive oil
- ³/₄ cup chopped fresh mint
- 2 pounds fresh peas, shelled, or two 10-ounce packages frozen peas, thawed
- 1 medium celery rib, chopped
- 1 medium carrot, chopped
- 3 ounces thickly sliced prosciutto, chopped
- Salt and freshly ground pepper
- Freshly grated Parmigiano-Reggiano

In a medium skillet, cook the onion in the oil over medium heat until very tender and golden brown, about 10 minutes. Add ½ cup of the mint leaves and stir well. Scrape the mixture into the slow cooker.

Add the peas, celery, carrot, and prosciutto. Add water to cover by 1 inch. Cover and cook on low for 2 hours, or until the vegetables are soft. Let cool slightly. Puree the mixture in a food processor or blender, in batches, if necessary.

Gently reheat the soup, if needed, and stir in the remaining ¼ cup mint. Season with salt and pepper to taste. Serve hot, sprinkled with the cheese.

Zucchini Soup
with Mint and Pecorino

The refreshing taste of mint and the salty tang of Pecorino cheese lift this summertime soup out of the ordinary. For the best flavor, use small, firm zucchini. You can substitute yellow summer squash for the zucchini, if you like.

SERVES 6

1 large onion, chopped
3 tablespoons olive oil
1 pound potatoes, peeled and diced
1½ pounds small zucchini (see headnote)
4 cups Chicken Broth (page 46) or canned chicken broth
½ cup spaghetti broken into 1-inch pieces
Salt and freshly ground pepper
2 tablespoons finely chopped fresh mint
½ cup freshly grated Pecorino Romano

In a medium skillet, cook the onion in the oil over medium heat, stirring occasionally, until tender but not browned, about 10 minutes. If the onion starts to color, add a tablespoon or two of water and lower the heat slightly. Scrape the onion into the slow cooker.

Add the potatoes and stir well. Add the zucchini and broth. Cover and cook on low for 3 hours. Add the spaghetti and cook for 30 minutes more, or until tender.

Season with salt and pepper to taste. Just before serving, stir in the mint and cheese. Serve hot.

Zucchini and Tomato Soup with Pesto

You can use either homemade or store-bought pesto here. Adding the pesto just before serving maximizes the fresh flavor. I like to make this soup with whole wheat pasta.

SERVES 8

- 1 medium onion, finely chopped
- 1 garlic clove, chopped
- 1 teaspoon chopped fresh rosemary
- 1 teaspoon chopped fresh sage
- 3 tablespoons olive oil
- 2 cups peeled, seeded, and chopped fresh or canned tomatoes
- 2 pounds zucchini, chopped
- 4 cups Chicken Broth (page 46) or canned chicken broth
- 4 cups water
- Salt and freshly ground pepper
- 1½ cups small pasta, such as elbows, ditali, or tubetti (see headnote)
- ¼ cup Basil Pesto (page 125) or store-bought
- ½ cup freshly grated Parmigiano-Reggiano

In a medium skillet, cook the onion, garlic, rosemary, and sage in the oil over medium heat until the onion is tender, about 10 minutes.

Scrape the onion mixture into a large slow cooker. Add the tomatoes, zucchini, broth, and water. Cover and cook on low for 5 hours, or until the zucchini is tender. Season to taste with salt and pepper.

Stir in the pasta. Cook for 20 minutes more, or until the pasta is tender. Just before serving, stir in the pesto and cheese.

Tomato Soup with Burrata or Goat Cheese

Imagine a soft, fresh, juicy mozzarella stuffed with a creamy cheese, and you have burrata, a luscious cheese from southern Italy that has recently become available here. Look for it at better cheese shops. If you can't find it, substitute a slice of creamy fresh goat cheese.

A food mill makes it easy to remove the seeds and skins from the cooked tomatoes. If you don't have one, peel and seed the tomatoes before cooking them.

SERVES 6

- 3 pounds very ripe tomatoes
- 2 tablespoons olive oil
- 1 medium onion, chopped
- 1 1/2 cups water
- Salt and freshly ground pepper
- 8 ounces burrata cheese (see page 11) or fresh goat cheese
- 4 fresh basil leaves, rolled and sliced crosswise

Cut the tomatoes in half lengthwise and remove the stem ends. Cut each tomato half into 4 pieces.

In a slow cooker, combine the tomatoes, oil, onion, water, and salt and pepper to taste. Cover and cook on low for 3 hours, or until the tomatoes are soft.

Let the soup cool slightly. Place a food mill over a large bowl. Pass the soup through the food mill to remove the seeds and skins. Reheat the soup, if necessary, and taste for seasoning.

Slice the burrata or goat cheese. Ladle the soup into bowls and top each portion with a slice of cheese. Scatter the basil on top and serve hot.

Cauliflower, Pancetta, and Pasta Soup

Ditalini and tubetti, little pasta tubes, are ideal for soup, since they fit well on a spoon. Pancetta and chopped garlic contribute extra flavor to this simple soup.

SERVES 8

2 ounces finely chopped pancetta (see page 13)

2 tablespoons olive oil

2 garlic cloves, finely chopped

1 medium cauliflower, about 1½ pounds, cut into ½-inch pieces

6 cups Chicken Broth (page 46) or canned chicken broth

Salt and freshly ground pepper

1½ cups ditalini or tubetti

¼ cup chopped fresh parsley

In a medium skillet, cook the pancetta in the oil over medium heat for 10 minutes, or until lightly golden. Add the garlic and cook for 1 minute more.

Scrape the mixture into a large slow cooker. Add the cauliflower and stir well.

Add the broth and salt and pepper to taste. Cover and cook on low for 6 hours, or until the cauliflower is very tender.

Stir in the pasta and cook for 30 minutes more, or until it is tender. Add the parsley just before serving. Serve hot.

Tomato, Barley, and Pecorino Soup

Chewy grains of barley are a pleasant and surprising change from pasta or rice.

SERVES 6

- 1 medium onion, finely chopped
- 2 tablespoons olive oil
- 6 cups Meat Broth (page 47) or canned beef broth
- 1 cup pearl barley, rinsed and picked over
- 2 medium tomatoes, peeled, seeded, and finely chopped, or 1 cup chopped canned tomatoes
- 1 medium celery rib, finely chopped
  Salt and freshly ground pepper
- 1 cup diced Pecorino Romano
- 2 tablespoons chopped fresh parsley

In a medium skillet, cook the onion in the oil over medium heat, stirring occasionally, until tender but not browned, about 10 minutes. If the onion starts to color, add a tablespoon or two of water and lower the heat slightly. Scrape the onion into a large slow cooker.

Add the broth, barley, tomatoes, and celery. Cover and cook for 3 hours on low, or until the barley is tender and the soup is thick.

Add salt and pepper to taste. Stir in the cheese and parsley. Serve hot.

Sicilian Lentil, Vegetable, and Pasta Soup

This is the kind of soup that welcomes improvisation. Try adding a couple of chopped potatoes or 2 cups chopped green beans, winter squash, or spinach leaves—whatever is in season or you happen to have on hand. I like to serve the soup with toasted Italian bread topped with thin slices of prosciutto di Parma.

SERVES 6

- 1 pound brown lentils, rinsed and picked over
- 1 large onion, chopped
- 2 medium carrots, chopped
- 1 large celery rib with leaves, chopped
- 2 large tomatoes, peeled, seeded, and chopped, or 1 cup chopped canned tomatoes
- 2 medium zucchini, yellow squash, or pattypan squash, chopped
- 6 cups water
- 1 cup ditalini, tubetti, or elbows
- Salt and freshly ground pepper
- Freshly grated Pecorino Romano

In a large slow cooker, combine the lentils, vegetables, and water.

Cover and cook on low for 7 hours. Add the pasta and salt and pepper to taste. Cook on high for 30 minutes more, or until the pasta is tender.

Serve hot, sprinkled with the cheese.

Milan-Style Pasta and Beans

I first tasted this soup in Milan, where it was made with *maltagliati*, leftover scraps of homemade pasta. You can use cut-up pieces of fresh fettuccine or even a small dried pasta shape, such as elbows or tubetti.

SERVES 8

- 2 tablespoons unsalted butter
- 2 tablespoons olive oil
- 6 fresh sage leaves, finely chopped
- 1 tablespoon chopped fresh rosemary
- 4 medium carrots, chopped
- 4 medium celery ribs, chopped
- 3 medium boiling potatoes, chopped
- 2 medium onions, chopped
- 4 medium tomatoes, peeled, seeded, and chopped, or 2 cups chopped canned tomatoes
- 1 recipe Basic Beans (page 191), or four 16-ounce cans cannellini beans with liquid

  About 3 cups Meat Broth (page 47) or canned beef broth

  Salt and freshly ground pepper
- 8 ounces fresh fettuccine, cut into 1-inch pieces

  Extra-virgin olive oil for drizzling

In a large pot, melt the butter with the oil over medium heat. Stir in the sage and rosemary. Add the carrots, celery, potatoes, and onions. Cook, stirring often, until softened, about 10 minutes. Transfer the mixture to a slow cooker.

Stir in the tomatoes and beans. Add the broth and salt and pepper to taste. Cook on low until all the ingredients are very tender, about 6 hours.

Turn the slow cooker to high. Remove half of the soup and pass it through a food mill or puree it in a blender. Pour the puree back into the slow cooker. Stir well and add the pasta. Cover and cook until the pasta is tender, about 30 minutes.

Serve hot, with a drizzle of olive oil and a generous grinding of pepper.

Spinach, Lentil, and Rice Soup

The Umbria region of central Italy produces *lenticchie di Castelluccio*, small brown lentils with a deep earthy flavor. They are delicious in this soup, though ordinary brown lentils will work well too.

SERVES 8 TO 10

- 1 pound brown lentils (see headnote), rinsed and picked over
- 4 large garlic cloves, chopped
- 2 medium celery ribs, chopped
- 2 medium carrots, chopped
- 7 cups water
- 1 cup white rice
- Salt and freshly ground pepper
- 10 ounces spinach, stemmed and torn into bite-size pieces
- Extra-virgin olive oil

In a slow cooker, combine the lentils, garlic, celery, carrots, and 6 cups of the water. Add more water, if needed, to cover the ingredients by ½ inch. Cover and cook on low for 7 hours.

Add the rice, the remaining 1 cup water, and salt and pepper to taste. Cover and cook for 30 minutes, or until the rice is tender. Stir in the spinach and cook for 15 minutes more.

Ladle into bowls, drizzle with olive oil, and grind on some black pepper.

Pasta Fagioli

Is this a pasta dish or a thick soup? I think of it as a thick soup. For a thinner texture, add a little water or broth.

SERVES 6

- 1 medium celery rib, chopped
- 2 garlic cloves, finely chopped
- ¼ cup olive oil
- 1 cup peeled, seeded, and chopped fresh or canned tomatoes
- 1 tablespoon tomato paste
- 2½ cups water
- 4 cups Basic Beans (page 191), or two 16-ounce cans cannellini or Great Northern beans with liquid
- Salt
- Pinch of crushed red pepper
- 8 ounces tubetti, elbows, or spaghetti broken into short pieces

In a small skillet, cook the celery and garlic in the oil over medium heat until the garlic is golden, about 2 minutes.

Scrape the mixture into the slow cooker. Add the tomatoes, tomato paste, and water and stir well. Add the beans, salt to taste, and crushed red pepper. Cover and cook on low for 4 hours.

Add the pasta and stir well. Cover and cook for 30 minutes more, or until the pasta is tender. Serve hot.

Tuscan Kale and Cannellini Soup with Garlic Croutons

Tuscan kale is only one of several names for this tasty heirloom variety. You may see it labeled as lacinato kale, black kale, or dinosaur kale. Its large, wrinkly, dark blue-green leaves are more tender and flavorful than other varieties. You can substitute collards, mustard greens, Swiss chard, or escarole, if you prefer.

SERVES 6

- 2 medium onions, chopped
- 2 tablespoons olive oil
- 2 garlic cloves, finely chopped
- 4 cups Basic Beans (page 191), or two 16-ounce cans cannellini beans with liquid
- 1 cup peeled, seeded, and chopped fresh or canned tomatoes
- 3 cups Chicken Broth (page 46), Meat Broth (page 47), or canned chicken or beef broth
- 8 ounces Tuscan kale (see headnote), cut into bite-size pieces
- 4 fresh sage leaves, chopped, or 2 teaspoons dried
  Salt and freshly ground pepper
  Extra-virgin olive oil for drizzling

CROUTONS

- 6 ½-inch-thick slices Italian or French bread
- 1–2 large garlic cloves, peeled

In a medium skillet, cook the onions in the oil over medium heat, stirring occasionally, until tender but not browned, about 10 minutes. If the onions start to color, add a tablespoon or two of water and lower the heat slightly. Stir in the garlic and cook for 2 minutes more. Scrape the mixture into the slow cooker.

In a food processor or blender, puree the beans until smooth. (If you like a coarser texture, just mash them with a potato masher.)

Add the pureed beans, the tomatoes, broth, kale, and sage to the cooker and stir well. Cover and cook on high for 3 hours or on low for 5 hours, or until the vegetables are tender. Add salt and pepper to taste. If the soup is too thick, thin it with a little water.

Just before serving, toast the bread and rub both sides with the garlic. Place the croutons in the serving bowls. Pour the soup over the bread and serve hot with a drizzle of olive oil.

Tuscan Bean and Farro Soup

Tuscan bean soups are legion, but this one just may be the best of all. It is a favorite in Lucca, a small city near the coast of Tuscany. The beans are cooked until the soup is thick and are then partially mashed. Farro, an ancient type of whole grain similar to wheat or spelt, has recently become popular again because it has a wonderful nutty quality and is highly nutritious.

Serve this as the Tuscans do, with a drizzle of extra-virgin olive oil on top.

SERVES 8

2 tablespoons olive oil

4 ounces pancetta (see page 13), diced

1 medium onion, chopped

2 medium celery ribs, chopped

2 medium carrots, chopped

2 garlic cloves, finely chopped

4 fresh sage leaves, chopped, or 2 teaspoons dried

1/2 teaspoon dried marjoram

6 cups cooked cannellini or Great Northern beans (see Basic Beans, page 191), or three 16-ounce cans beans with liquid

1 cup peeled, seeded, and chopped fresh or canned tomatoes

Salt and freshly ground pepper

1 cup farro (see page 12)

Extra-virgin olive oil for drizzling

In a large skillet, heat the oil over medium heat. Add the pancetta and cook for 5 minutes, or until lightly browned. Add the onion, celery, and carrots and cook, stirring often, until softened. Stir in the garlic, sage, and marjoram.

Scrape the vegetables into the slow cooker. Add the beans, tomatoes, and a pinch of salt and pepper. Cover and cook on low for 6 hours, or until the vegetables are tender.

With a slotted spoon or a strainer, transfer the beans and vegetables to a bowl. Leave the cooker on.

Let the bean mixture cool slightly. Place in a food processor and puree. The mixture should not be completely smooth. Scrape it back into the slow cooker. Taste for seasoning. Add the farro and cover. Cook for 1 to 2 hours more, or until the farro is tender. Serve hot with a drizzle of olive oil.

Chickpea and Porcini Soup

The woodsy flavor of dried porcini mushrooms and the meatiness of pancetta add character to this soup.

An immersion or stick blender is ideal for pureeing foods right in the slow cooker. It saves you from having to let the soup cool, transferring the contents of the cooker to a blender or food processor, and then reheating it.

SERVES 6

- 1 ounce dried porcini mushrooms or other dried mushrooms
- 1 cup hot water
- 2 ounces chopped pancetta (see page 13)
- 2 small celery ribs, chopped
- 2 large carrots, chopped
- 1 large onion, chopped
- 2 tablespoons olive oil
- 1 pound cooked chickpeas with their liquid (see Basic Beans, page 191), or three 16-ounce cans chickpeas with liquid
- 2 large tomatoes, peeled, seeded, and chopped, or 2 cups chopped canned tomatoes with their juice
- Extra-virgin olive oil for drizzling

CROUTONS

- 6 ½-inch-thick slices Italian or French bread
- 1–2 large garlic cloves, peeled

Place the dried porcini in a bowl with the hot water. Let stand for 30 minutes. Lift the porcini out of the water and squeeze them to extract more liquid. If the water seems gritty, filter it through a piece of cheesecloth or a paper coffee filter. Set the soaking liquid aside. Chop the porcini.

In a large skillet, cook the pancetta, celery, carrots, and onion in the oil, stirring often, until tender and golden, about 20 minutes. Scrape the mixture into the slow cooker and add the chickpeas, tomatoes, porcini, and soaking liquid. Add water, if needed, to just cover the ingredients.

Cover and cook on low for 4 hours, or until the vegetables are soft. Pour the soup into a blender or food processor, in batches if necessary, and process until smooth. Reheat the soup gently on low heat, if needed.

Just before serving, toast the bread and rub the slices on both sides with the garlic. Place the croutons in the serving bowls. Pour the soup over the bread and serve hot with a drizzle of olive oil.

Calamari Soup

An abundance of vegetables and fresh basil or parsley make this seafood soup colorful and fresh tasting.

SERVES 6

- 1 medium green bell pepper, chopped
- 2 large garlic cloves, chopped
- 1/4 cup olive oil
- 1 1/2 pounds cleaned calamari, cut into 1/2-inch rings
- 1 cup peeled, seeded, and chopped fresh or canned tomatoes
- 1 large carrot, chopped
- 2 medium celery ribs, chopped
- 2 medium potatoes, diced
- 1 8-ounce bottle clam juice
- 5 cups water
- 2 cups fresh or thawed frozen peas
- 1 cup white rice
  Salt and freshly ground pepper
- 2 tablespoons chopped fresh basil or parsley

In a large skillet, cook the bell pepper and garlic in the oil over medium heat until tender, about 15 minutes. Scrape the mixture into a large slow cooker.

Add the calamari, tomatoes, carrot, celery, potatoes, clam juice, and water. Cover and cook on low for 2 hours. Add the peas, rice, and salt and pepper to taste. Cover and cook for 20 minutes more, or until the rice is tender. Stir in the basil or parsley and serve hot.

Chicken and Orzo Soup

Kids adore this simple soup. You can substitute dark meat for the chicken breasts, if you prefer.

SERVES 6

8 cups Chicken Broth (page 46) or canned chicken broth

1 medium onion, finely chopped

2 large carrots, chopped

2 medium celery ribs, chopped

1½ pounds boneless, skinless chicken breasts, cut into ½-inch chunks

2 medium zucchini, chopped

1 cup orzo or another small pasta shape

1 cup thawed frozen peas

Salt and freshly ground pepper

½ cup freshly grated Parmigiano-Reggiano

¼ cup chopped fresh basil or parsley

In a slow cooker, combine the broth, onion, carrots, and celery. Cover and cook on low for 3 hours.

Add the chicken, zucchini, orzo, and peas. Cook for 30 minutes, or until the orzo is tender and the chicken is cooked through. Season to taste with salt and pepper. Stir in the cheese and basil or parsley and serve hot.

Turkey Meatball and Escarole Soup

Escarole, a member of the endive family of greens, has chewy leaves and a slightly bitter flavor that becomes sweet and mellow as it cooks. You can use it raw in a salad or sauté it, but it is at its best in soup. Substitute spinach or Swiss chard if you can't find escarole.

SERVES 8

- 3 large carrots, chopped
- 10 cups Chicken Broth (page 46) or canned chicken broth
- ½ pound escarole (half a head), washed and cut into bite-size pieces (see headnote)
- 1 pound ground turkey
- 1 small onion, minced
- 2 large eggs, beaten
- ½ cup plain dry bread crumbs
- ½ cup freshly grated Parmigiano-Reggiano, plus more for serving
- 1 teaspoon salt
- ¼ teaspoon freshly ground pepper

In a large slow cooker, combine the carrots and broth. Stir in the escarole. Cover and cook on low for 4 hours.

In a medium bowl, combine the turkey, onion, eggs, bread crumbs, cheese, salt, and pepper. Mix well and shape into 1-inch meatballs. Carefully place the meatballs into the soup. Cover and cook for 4 hours more, or until the meatballs are cooked through. Serve hot, sprinkled with additional cheese.

Chicken Broth

Homemade broth is easy to make in a slow cooker. It keeps in the refrigerator for several days and freezes well. It costs a fraction of store-bought, tastes better, and, because it is low in sodium and has no artificial ingredients, is better for you.

For a richer-flavored broth, use a few turkey wings in place of some of the chicken. I generally don't salt the broth, preferring, instead, to salt the dish to which it will be added.

MAKES 2½ QUARTS

- 3 pounds chicken wings, backs, or other parts (see headnote)
- 1 large onion, peeled
- 2 medium celery ribs with leaves, coarsely chopped
- 1 large carrot, coarsely chopped
- 6 whole peppercorns
- A few fresh parsley sprigs
- 10 cups water

Combine all the ingredients in a large slow cooker. Cover and cook on low for 8 hours.

Let cool slightly. Strain the broth into a bowl and discard the solids. Refrigerate until cold. Remove the fat from the surface.

Use within 3 days or freeze for up to 6 months.

Meat Broth

This broth is easy in a slow cooker, has no additives or preservatives, as do many processed broths, and keeps well in the freezer. And, if you're careful about saving meat scraps, it costs practically nothing to make. Use this broth in soups, sauces, and risottos.

MAKES 2½ QUARTS

- 3 pounds meaty beef bones
- 1 pound chicken or turkey wings
- 1 large onion, peeled
- 2 medium carrots, cut into chunks
- 2 medium celery ribs, cut into chunks
- ½ cup chopped fresh parsley

Combine all the ingredients in a large slow cooker. Add water to cover by 1 inch. Cover and cook on low for 8 to 10 hours.

Let cool slightly. Strain the broth into a bowl and discard the solids. Refrigerate the broth until cold, then scrape the fat off the surface.

Use within 3 days or freeze for up to 6 months.

Sauces
for Pasta

Sauces for Pasta

Sweet Tomato Sauce

Ripe tomatoes are naturally sweet. The only reason to add sugar is to mask the flavor of unripe or poor-quality tomatoes. Try this sauce with meaty, summer-ripe tomatoes and see what I mean.

Serve with a fresh egg pasta such as fettuccine or with potato gnocchi.

MAKES 4 CUPS

- 5 pounds ripe plum tomatoes
- 2 medium carrots, coarsely chopped
- 1 large red onion, coarsely chopped
  Salt
  Extra-virgin olive oil
- 6 fresh basil leaves, torn into bits

Bring a large pot of water to a boil. Add a few of the tomatoes and cook for 30 seconds. Remove with a slotted spoon and let cool. Repeat with the remaining tomatoes.

Peel the tomatoes, then cut them in half lengthwise and gently squeeze out the seeds and juice. Coarsely chop the tomatoes.

Combine the tomatoes, carrots, and onion in a large slow cooker. Add a pinch of salt. Cover and cook on low for 6 hours or on high for 3 hours, or until the vegetables are tender.

Let the sauce cool slightly. Puree it in a food processor or blender. Taste for seasoning. This sauce keeps well in the refrigerator for up to 3 days or in the freezer for up to 6 months. Just before serving, reheat gently, if needed. Stir in the olive oil and basil.

Tomato and Red Wine Sauce

Meat loaf, pasta, vegetables, and omelets all benefit from this flavorful sauce. Store it in the freezer to spice up meals anytime.

MAKES 6 CUPS

- 1 medium onion, chopped
- 1/3 cup olive oil
- 2 garlic cloves, minced
- 1 cup dry red wine
- 2 28-ounce cans tomato puree
- Salt and freshly ground pepper
- 10 fresh basil leaves

In a medium skillet, cook the onion in the oil over medium heat, stirring occasionally, until tender but not browned, about 10 minutes. If the onion starts to color, add a tablespoon or two of water and lower the heat slightly. Stir in the garlic and cook for 2 minutes more. Add the wine and bring it to a simmer. Pour the mixture into the slow cooker.

Add the tomato puree and salt and pepper to taste. Cover and cook on high for 2 hours or on low for 4 hours, or until the sauce is thick.

Just before serving, tear the basil into small pieces and stir it into the sauce. Refrigerate for up to 3 days or freeze for up to 6 months.

Fresh Tomato Puree

Use very ripe, meaty tomatoes to make this simple puree. I prepare it in large batches and freeze it in 1- and 2-cup portions to use in soups, sauces, and stews all year. It lends itself to many variations: for example, add a chopped red bell pepper, a carrot, a tender celery rib, herbs, or a small fresh chile to the tomatoes.

MAKES 4 CUPS

- 4 pounds very ripe tomatoes
- 1 medium onion, coarsely chopped

Cut the tomatoes in half lengthwise. Cut out the stem ends.

Place the onion in the slow cooker and add the tomatoes. Cook on low for 3 hours, or until the tomatoes are very tender. Let cool slightly.

Pass the tomato mixture through the fine holes of a food mill. Discard the solids. Transfer the tomato puree to plastic containers and seal tightly. Refrigerate for up to 3 days or freeze for up to 6 months.

Gardener's Sauce

A garden full of vegetables takes the place of meat in this spicy, summery pasta sauce. There is quite a lot of chopping to do, but most of it can be done in the food processor. Serve with fettuccine, penne, or bow ties and grated Parmigiano-Reggiano.

MAKES 5 CUPS

- 2 medium onions, finely chopped
- 1 tablespoon finely chopped garlic
- 1 tablespoon finely chopped fresh rosemary
- 1 tablespoon finely chopped fresh thyme
- Pinch of crushed red pepper
- 1/3 cup olive oil
- 1/2 cup dry white wine
- 2 small zucchini, finely chopped
- 1 medium eggplant, finely chopped
- 1 medium carrot, finely chopped
- 1 medium celery rib, finely chopped
- Salt and freshly ground pepper
- 1/4 cup chopped fresh basil or parsley

In a medium skillet, cook the onions, garlic, herbs, and crushed red pepper in the oil over medium heat, stirring occasionally, until tender but not browned, about 10 minutes. If the onions start to color, add a tablespoon or two of water and lower the heat slightly. Add the wine and simmer for 1 minute. Scrape the mixture into the slow cooker.

Add the remaining vegetables and salt and pepper to taste. Cook on high for 3 hours or on low for 6 hours, or until the vegetables are soft. If the sauce looks too thin, remove the cover for the last 30 minutes. Stir in the basil or parsley.

Seafood Sauce

Fresh basil complements the seafood flavors in this sauce. Serve with spaghetti, linguine, or other thin pasta strands.

MAKES 10 CUPS

- 1 large onion, finely chopped
- 6 garlic cloves, finely chopped
- 1/3 cup olive oil
- 1/4 cup chopped fresh parsley
- 1 pound cleaned calamari, cut into 1/2-inch rings
  Salt
- 1/2 cup dry white wine
- 2 28-ounce cans tomato puree
- 1/2 pound shelled and deveined medium shrimp, cut into 3 or 4 pieces
  Pinch of crushed red pepper (optional)
- 1 pound small clams, soaked and scrubbed
- 1 pound mussels, soaked and scrubbed
- 6 large fresh basil leaves, torn into bits, or 3 tablespoons chopped fresh parsley

In a medium skillet, cook the onion and garlic in the oil over medium heat until tender and golden, about 10 minutes. Stir in the parsley.

Rinse the calamari and pat dry. Add the calamari and a pinch of salt to the skillet. Add the wine and bring the mixture to a simmer.

Pour the tomato puree into a large slow cooker. Add the contents of the skillet. Cover and cook on low for 3 hours.

Stir in the shrimp and crushed red pepper, if using. Add the clams and mussels, pressing them into the sauce. Cover and cook for 20 minutes more, or until the shells open. Remove the shells, if desired. Stir in the basil or parsley.

Sicilian Swordfish Ragu

Sicilians cook swordfish in dozens of ways. In this ragu, it is simmered in a tasty tomato sauce, much as you would cook ground meat. Serve with cavatelli pasta.

MAKES 8 CUPS

- 3 medium celery ribs, chopped
- 2 medium carrots, chopped
- 4 garlic cloves, finely chopped
- 2 tablespoons finely chopped fresh parsley
- 1/4 cup olive oil
- 2 28-ounce cans Italian peeled tomatoes with their juice, chopped
  Salt
- 1 pound swordfish, skin removed
- 1/2 cup pitted and chopped Sicilian green olives
- 1/4 cup rinsed, drained, and chopped capers
- 1/2 teaspoon dried oregano
  Pinch of crushed red pepper

In a large skillet, cook the celery, carrots, garlic, and parsley in the oil over medium heat, stirring occasionally, until golden. Scrape the vegetables into the slow cooker. Add the tomatoes and salt to taste. Cover and cook on low for 3 to 4 hours, or until thick.

Cut the swordfish into 1/2-inch pieces. Add the fish, olives, capers, oregano, and crushed red pepper to the slow cooker and stir well. Cover and cook for 1 hour more, or until the fish is tender.

Chicken Ragu

Chicken, herbs, wine, and tomato simmer into a thick, rich sauce for pasta. I prefer chicken legs and thighs for this ragu. Dark meat has more moisture and flavor, so it doesn't dry out, and it keeps its flavor during the long, slow cooking.

SERVES 8

- 2 tablespoons olive oil
- 6 chicken thighs and drumsticks, skin on
- 1 medium onion, chopped
- 2 medium carrots, chopped
- 1 medium celery rib, chopped
- 2 garlic cloves, finely chopped
- ½ cup dry white wine
- 1 28-ounce can tomato puree
- 2 tablespoons tomato paste
- 1 tablespoon finely chopped fresh thyme
- 1 tablespoon finely chopped fresh sage
- Salt and freshly ground pepper

In a large skillet, heat the oil over medium-high heat and brown the chicken pieces on all sides. Transfer the chicken to the slow cooker.

Reduce the heat to medium and add the onion, carrots, celery, and garlic to the skillet. Cook, stirring frequently, until the vegetables are lightly golden, about 10 minutes. Add the wine and bring it to a simmer. Scrape the mixture into the slow cooker.

Stir in the tomato puree, tomato paste, herbs, and salt and pepper to taste. Cover and cook on high for 2 hours or on low for 4 hours, or until the chicken pulls away from the bone. Remove the chicken and let cool slightly. Discard the skin and bones and cut the chicken into bite-size pieces. Return the chicken to the sauce.

Just before serving, reheat the sauce if necessary.

Meat and Mushroom Ragu

Italian cooks often use dried porcini mushrooms to add a deep, woodsy flavor to pasta sauces, soups, and stews. But porcini have become very expensive in recent years, so I often substitute other varieties of dried mushrooms, such as shiitake or black mushrooms. Their flavor is not quite as elegant as porcini, but it is still very good.

MAKES 12 CUPS

1½ ounces dried porcini or other wild mushrooms (see headnote)

2 cups hot water

2 tablespoons unsalted butter

2 tablespoons olive oil

1 medium onion, chopped

2 medium carrots, chopped

2 medium celery ribs, chopped

8 ounces mushrooms of your choice, chopped

3 garlic cloves, finely chopped

1 pound ground beef chuck

3 sweet Italian pork sausages, casings removed

Salt and freshly ground pepper

Place the dried mushrooms in a bowl with the hot water. Let stand for 30 minutes. Lift the mushrooms out of the water and squeeze them to extract more liquid. If the water seems gritty, filter it through a piece of cheesecloth or a paper coffee filter. Set the soaking liquid aside. Chop the mushrooms and set aside.

In a large skillet, melt the butter with the oil over medium heat. Add the onion, carrots, celery, fresh mushrooms, and garlic and cook, stirring often, until golden. Add the beef and sausage and cook, stirring frequently to break up any lumps, until browned.

Scrape the mixture into the slow cooker. Add the reconstituted mushrooms, the soaking liquid, and salt and pepper to taste.

Cover and cook on low for 4 to 6 hours, or until the sauce is thick.

Turkey Ragu alla Bolognese

Bolognese-style ragu is typically made with ground veal or beef, but turkey makes a flavorful substitute. A bit of cream added to the sauce rounds out the flavor and smooths the texture. Serve over fresh spinach or egg fettuccine with grated Parmigiano-Reggiano.

MAKES 10 CUPS

- 2 tablespoons unsalted butter
- 2 tablespoons olive oil
- 1 medium onion, finely chopped
- 2 medium celery ribs, finely chopped
- 2 medium carrots, finely chopped
- 2 garlic cloves, finely chopped
- 4 ounces pancetta (see page 13), chopped
- 1½ pounds ground turkey
- 2 tablespoons tomato paste
- 1 cup dry white wine
- 1 cup Chicken Broth (page 46) or canned chicken broth
- 1 28-ounce can Italian peeled tomatoes, drained and finely chopped
- ½ teaspoon freshly grated nutmeg
- Salt and freshly ground pepper
- ½ cup heavy cream

In a large saucepan, melt the butter with the oil over medium heat. Add the onion, celery, carrots, and garlic and cook until tender and golden, about 20 minutes. Stir in the pancetta and ground turkey and cook, stirring often, until browned, about 15 minutes. Stir in the tomato paste, wine, and broth and bring to a simmer.

Scrape the mixture into the slow cooker and add the tomatoes, nutmeg, and salt and pepper to taste. Cover and cook on low for 6 hours, or until thick. Stir in the cream and cook for 15 minutes more.

Spicy Tuscan Sausage Ragu

This thick, rich sauce is heavenly on chunky cuts of pasta, such as rigatoni or rotelle. You can adjust the spice level by using more or less hot sausage.

MAKES 10 CUPS

- 2 tablespoons olive oil
- 1 pound sweet Italian pork sausage, casings removed
- ½ pound hot Italian pork sausage, casings removed
- 1 large red onion, finely chopped
- 2 garlic cloves, finely chopped
- ½ cup dry red wine
- 1 28-ounce can Italian peeled tomatoes with their juice, chopped
- 1 28-ounce can tomato puree
  Salt
- 1 cup heavy cream

In a large skillet, heat the oil over medium heat. Crumble the sausages into the pan and cook, stirring frequently to break up the lumps, until the meat is lightly browned. Add the onion and garlic and cook until the onion is tender.

Add the wine and scrape the bottom of the skillet. Pour the contents into the slow cooker. Add the tomatoes, puree, and a pinch of salt. Cover and cook on low for 5 hours. Stir in the cream and cook for 1 hour more, or until the meat is very tender. Taste for seasoning.

The Butcher's Sauce

Whenever I do a lot of cooking, my freezer collects an assortment of small quantities of different meats, such as a half pound of ground beef, a pork chop, an extra sausage, or a chicken breast. I chop the meats in the food processor and make this delicious pasta sauce, which in Puglia, in southern Italy, is known as the butcher's sauce.

Don't hesitate to use a different combination of meats according to what you have on hand. Serve as they do in Puglia, with orecchiette, cavatelli, or another chunky pasta.

MAKES ABOUT 10 CUPS

- 1 large onion, chopped
- 2 medium celery ribs, chopped
- 2 medium carrots, chopped
- 2 garlic cloves, minced
- 3 tablespoons olive oil
- 1/2 pound ground beef
- 1/2 pound ground pork
- 1/2 pound ground lamb
- 2 tablespoons tomato paste
- Salt and freshly ground pepper
- 1/2 cup dry white wine
- 2 28-ounce cans Italian peeled tomatoes packed in tomato puree, chopped

In a large skillet over medium heat, cook the vegetables in the oil, stirring often, until tender and golden but not browned, about 10 minutes. If the onion starts to color, add a tablespoon or two of water and lower the heat slightly.

Add the meats and cook, breaking up lumps with the back of a spoon, until lightly browned. Stir in the tomato paste and salt and pepper to taste. Add the wine and bring the mixture to a simmer.

Pour the tomatoes into a large slow cooker. Scrape the meat and vegetables into the cooker and stir well. Cover and cook on high for 4 hours or on low for 8 hours, or until the sauce is thick.

Chunky Pork Shoulder Ragu

The pork shoulder roast practically melts into this flavorful sauce. A hearty pasta like rigatoni is the perfect choice, and the ragu is also good on polenta.

MAKES ABOUT 10 CUPS

- 2 tablespoons olive oil
- 2 pounds boneless pork shoulder roast, rolled and tied
- Salt and freshly ground pepper
- 1 medium onion, chopped
- 1/2 teaspoon fennel seeds
- 4 large garlic cloves, finely chopped
- 1 tablespoon finely chopped fresh sage
- 1 teaspoon finely chopped fresh rosemary
- 1 28-ounce can tomato puree
- 1 28-ounce can Italian peeled tomatoes, drained and chopped
- Salt
- Pinch of crushed red pepper
- 1/2 cup chopped fresh basil

In a large skillet, heat the oil over medium heat. Sprinkle the meat with salt and pepper and brown it on all sides. Remove the meat to a large slow cooker.

Add the onion and fennel seeds to the skillet and cook until the onion is tender and golden, about 10 minutes. Stir in the garlic, sage, and rosemary. Add the tomato puree, tomatoes, and a pinch of salt and stir well. Pour the sauce into the slow cooker. Add the crushed red pepper. Cover and cook on low for 5 to 6 hours, or until the pork is very tender.

Remove the meat to a cutting board but leave the sauce in the slow cooker with the heat on. With two forks, tear the pork into bite-size pieces. Return the pork to the cooker to reheat. Stir in the basil.

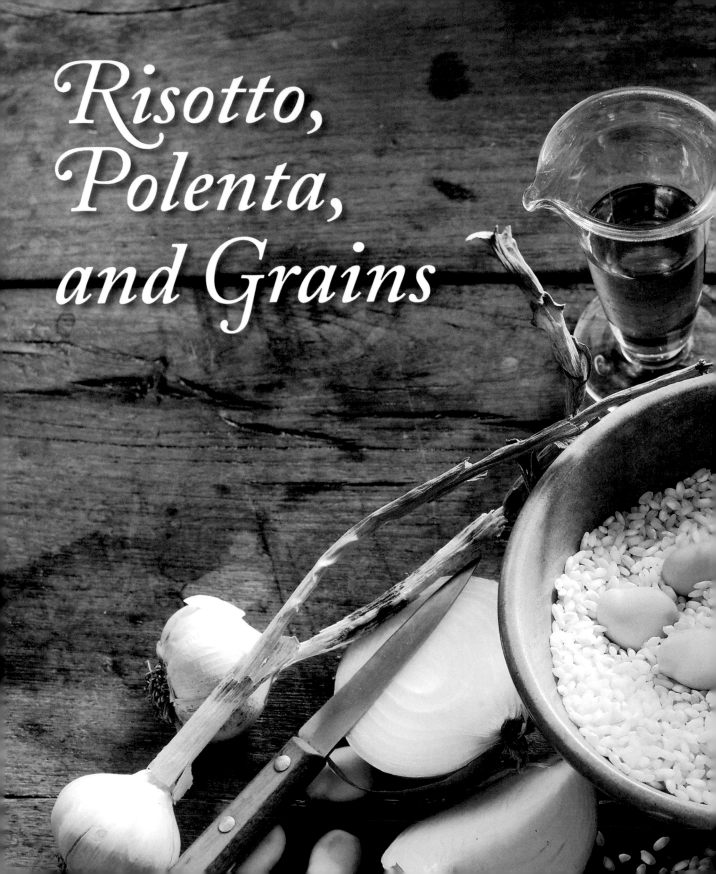

Risotto, Polenta, and Grains

Risotto, Polenta, and Grains

Green Risotto

In Italy, risotto is served as a first course, like soup or pasta. Risotto made in the slow cooker requires little or no attention, so it is an ideal side dish for chicken or fish.

SERVES 6 TO 8

3 tablespoons unsalted butter

1 tablespoon olive oil

1 medium onion, finely chopped

2 cups short-grain rice, such as Arborio

4 cups Chicken Broth (page 46), canned chicken broth, or water
    Salt and freshly ground pepper

1 10-ounce package frozen chopped spinach, thawed

¼ cup chopped fresh parsley

¼ cup chopped fresh basil

½ cup freshly grated Parmigiano-Reggiano

In a large skillet, melt 2 tablespoons of the butter with the olive oil over medium heat. Add the onion and cook, stirring occasionally, until tender and golden, about 10 minutes. Add the rice. Cook and stir for 2 minutes, or until the rice is well coated. Scrape the mixture into the slow cooker.

Add the broth or water and salt and pepper to taste. Cook for 30 minutes on high. Stir in the spinach and cook for 30 minutes more, or until the rice is tender and the liquid is absorbed. If the rice seems dry, stir in a little warm water.

Stir in the parsley, basil, the remaining 1 tablespoon butter, and the cheese. Serve hot.

Risotto with Artichokes

As a variation, add some tender peas and fresh fava beans toward the end of the cooking time.

SERVES 6

- 3 tablespoons unsalted butter
- 1 tablespoon olive oil
- 1 medium onion, chopped
- 2 garlic cloves, finely chopped
- 2 cups short-grain rice, such as Arborio
- ½ cup dry white wine
- 1 10–12 ounce package frozen artichoke hearts, thawed
- 4 cups Chicken Broth (page 46), canned chicken broth, or water
- 2 tablespoons chopped fresh parsley
- Salt and freshly ground pepper
- ½ cup freshly grated Parmigiano-Reggiano

In a large skillet, melt 2 tablespoons of the butter with the oil over medium heat. Add the onion and cook until tender and golden, about 10 minutes. Stir in the garlic. Add the rice and cook, stirring occasionally, for 2 minutes. Add the wine and cook until the liquid evaporates. Scrape the mixture into the slow cooker.

Add the artichokes, broth or water, parsley, and salt and pepper to taste. Cover and cook on high for about 1 hour, or until the rice is tender. If the rice seems dry, stir in a little warm water.

Stir in the remaining 1 tablespoon butter and the cheese. Serve hot.

Three-Mushroom Risotto

Italians love mushrooms so much that in the fall, when wild ones are in season, some restaurants devote their whole menu to them. Risotto made with several varieties of mushrooms is typical. In this version, dried porcini add a deep woodsy richness to the more delicate flavors of the button and oyster mushrooms. Don't hesitate to substitute other varieties, if you prefer. I serve this risotto with grilled steak, roast beef, or beef pot roast.

SERVES 6 TO 8

- ½ cup dried porcini mushrooms
- 1 cup hot water
- 3 tablespoons unsalted butter
- 1 tablespoon olive oil
- ½ cup chopped shallots or onion
- 2 cups short-grain rice, such as Arborio
- ½ cup dry red wine
- 2 cups Meat Broth (page 47) or canned beef or vegetable broth
- 8 ounces button mushrooms, sliced
- 4 ounces oyster mushrooms, sliced
- Salt and freshly ground pepper
- ¾ cup freshly grated Parmigiano-Reggiano

Place the dried porcini in a bowl with the hot water. Let stand for 30 minutes. Lift the porcini out of the water and squeeze them to extract more liquid. If the water seems gritty, filter it through a piece of cheesecloth or a paper coffee filter. Set the soaking liquid aside. Chop the porcini and set aside.

In a large skillet, melt 2 tablespoons of the butter with the oil over medium heat. Add the shallots or onion and cook, stirring occasionally, until tender and golden, about 5 minutes. Add the rice. Cook and stir for 2 minutes, or until the rice is well coated. Add the wine and simmer until it evaporates. Scrape the mixture into the slow cooker.

Add the broth, porcini, soaking liquid, fresh mushrooms, and salt and pepper to taste. Cook on high for 1½ hours, stirring once, or until the rice is tender and the liquid is absorbed. If the rice seems dry, stir in a little warm water.

Stir in the remaining 1 tablespoon butter and the cheese. Serve hot.

Risotto with Calamari

Sturdy calamari are perfect for risotto, as they don't overcook.

SERVES 6

- 1 large onion, chopped
- 3 tablespoons olive oil
- 1 pound cleaned calamari (fresh or thawed frozen), cut into $\frac{1}{2}$-inch rings; tentacles halved through the base
- $\frac{1}{2}$ cup dry white wine
- 2 cups short-grain rice, such as Arborio
- 5 cups water
  Salt and freshly ground pepper
- 2 cups peeled, seeded, and chopped fresh or canned tomatoes
- 2 tablespoons chopped fresh parsley
  Extra-virgin olive oil for drizzling

In a large skillet, cook the onion in the oil over medium heat, stirring occasionally, until tender and golden, about 10 minutes. Stir in the calamari and wine. Cook for 1 minute.

Stir in the rice and cook, stirring, for 2 minutes. Scrape the mixture into a large slow cooker and add the water. Cover and cook on high for 1½ hours, or until the rice is tender. Season to taste with salt and pepper and stir in the tomatoes and parsley. If the rice seems dry, stir in a little warm water.

Serve hot, drizzled with the olive oil.

Basic Polenta

Making polenta the old-fashioned way involves a lot of stirring and attention, but cooking it in a slow cooker is a snap. Once the polenta is done, set the cooker to the warm setting to keep it soft and creamy until you are ready to serve it. Add a little liquid if it seems too thick or dry.

Polenta goes great with fried eggs, fish, or meat stews.

SERVES 6

1 cup coarsely ground yellow cornmeal, preferably stone-ground
1½ teaspoons salt
5 cups water
Water, milk, broth, or cream, if needed

In a large slow cooker, stir together the cornmeal, salt, and water. Cover and cook on high for 2 hours. Stir the polenta. If it seems too thick, add a little water, milk, broth, or cream. Cook for 30 to 60 minutes more, or until thick and creamy. Serve hot.

Variations

» Use half broth and half water.

» Use half milk and half water.

» Stir 2 tablespoons butter or olive oil into the finished polenta.

» Add herbs or grated cheese to the finished polenta.

Polenta with Broccoli

This is a fine side dish with stew or pot roast, or serve it instead of pasta, topped with Spicy Tuscan Sausage Ragu (page 63).

SERVES 8

1¼ cups coarsely ground yellow cornmeal, preferably stone-ground

1½ teaspoons salt

6 cups water

4 cups chopped broccoli florets (from 1 large bunch)

¾ cup freshly grated Parmigiano-Reggiano

¼ cup chopped fresh parsley

2 tablespoons unsalted butter

In a large slow cooker, stir together the cornmeal, salt, and water. Cover and cook on high for 2 hours. Stir in the broccoli. If the mixture seems too thick, stir in a little warm water. Cover and cook for 1 hour more, or until the broccoli is tender and the polenta is thick.

Stir in the cheese, parsley, and butter. Serve hot.

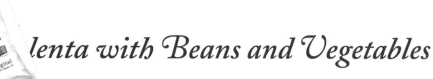

lenta with Beans and Vegetables

...is called "polenta in chains," because the strands of shredded veg-
...es are entwined throughout the polenta, giving it flavor and color.

Pack any leftovers into a small bowl and refrigerate until firm. When you are
ready to cook, slide the polenta out of the container and cut it into slices. Dust
the cut sides with flour and brown in olive oil or butter. Serve hot for breakfast
or brunch, topped with fried eggs.

SERVES 6 TO 8

5	cups water
1	cup coarsely ground yellow cornmeal, preferably stone-ground
1	garlic clove, very finely chopped
1½	teaspoons salt
1	cup shredded carrots
2	cups shredded kale, escarole, or spinach
2	cups cooked or canned cannellini beans (from a 15- or 16-ounce can), drained
	Freshly ground pepper
½	cup freshly grated Parmigiano-Reggiano
3	tablespoons olive oil

In a large slow cooker, stir together the water, cornmeal, garlic, and salt. Cover
and cook on high for 2 hours. Stir in the vegetables, beans, and pepper to taste.
Cover and cook until the polenta has absorbed all the liquid and the vegetables are
tender, 30 to 60 minutes more. Stir in the cheese and olive oil. Serve hot.

Creamy Polenta with Gorgonzola and Mascarpone

Polenta and cheese go together like bread and butter, and it doesn't get much better than this luscious combination made with earthy Gorgonzola and thick, creamy mascarpone. It is quite rich and can be served as a meatless main course with broccoli or asparagus.

SERVES 6 TO 8

- 2 cups water
- 2 cups milk
- 1 cup coarsely ground yellow cornmeal, preferably stone-ground
- 1/2 teaspoon salt
- 1/2 cup mascarpone cheese
- 1/2 cup crumbled Gorgonzola cheese

In a large slow cooker, stir together the water, milk, cornmeal, and salt. Cover and cook on high for 2 hours. Stir well and cook for 30 to 60 minutes more, or until the polenta is thick.

Turn off the cooker. Stir in the mascarpone and half of the Gorgonzola. Pour the polenta into a serving bowl. Sprinkle with the remaining Gorgonzola and serve hot.

Polenta with Pork Ragu

If you are looking for something comforting to eat, stop right here! Creamy golden polenta, lots of melted cheese, and a rich meat sauce make this what I think of as "happy" food. I serve it as a main course with a side of garlicky sautéed spinach or broccoli rabe.

SERVES 6 TO 8

- 1¼ cups coarsely ground yellow cornmeal, preferably stone-ground
- 1 teaspoon salt
- 6 cups water
- 2 tablespoons unsalted butter
- 6 ounces Asiago, fontina, or mozzarella cheese, sliced
- 3 cups Chunky Pork Shoulder Ragu (page 67) or other meat sauce
- ½ cup freshly grated Parmigiano-Reggiano

In a large slow cooker, stir together the cornmeal, salt, and water. Cover and cook on high for 2 hours. Stir well. Cover and cook for 30 to 60 minutes more, or until the polenta is thickened. If it seems too thick, stir in a little warm water.

Stir in the butter and smooth the surface. Arrange the cheese slices on top. Spoon on the sauce. Sprinkle with the grated cheese. Cover and cook for 30 minutes, or until the sauce is heated and the cheese is melted. Serve hot.

Barley with Spring Vegetables

Northern Italian cooks prepare barley like risotto and call the finished dish *orzotto*. This version has a springtime flavor from a variety of fresh vegetables. Serve as a side dish with roast chicken or as a meatless main dish.

SERVES 6

- 4 tablespoons (1/2 stick) unsalted butter
- 1 1/2 cups pearl barley, rinsed and picked over
- 1 medium onion, finely chopped
- 1 cup chopped celery
- 2 medium carrots, chopped
- 1/2 cup chopped red bell pepper
- 1 cup chopped mushrooms of your choice
- 3 cups Chicken Broth (page 46) or canned chicken broth
- 1 cup fresh or thawed frozen peas
- Salt and freshly ground pepper
- 1/4 cup freshly grated Parmigiano-Reggiano

In a slow cooker, combine 3 tablespoons of the butter, the barley, onion, celery, carrots, bell pepper, mushrooms, and broth. Cover and cook on high for 1 hour. Stir in the peas and salt and pepper to taste. Cook for 1 hour more, or until the barley is tender and the liquid is absorbed. If the barley is too dry, stir in a little warm water.

Stir in the remaining 1 tablespoon butter. Stir in the cheese. Serve hot.

Farro with Tomatoes, Basil, and Cheese

Farro is one of the oldest cultivated grains. A relative of wheat, it's usually cooked with broth in pilaf or soup. It has a warm, nutty flavor and chewy texture. Since it is a whole grain, it's very healthful. You can find farro at Italian markets and in many health food stores. This is good as a side dish with beef stew or an omelet or as a main dish with a green salad.

SERVES 8

- 1 medium onion, finely chopped
- 1½ teaspoons salt
- 2 cups cherry or grape tomatoes, halved or quartered if large
- 4 cups water
- 2 cups whole-grain farro (see page 12), rinsed and picked over
- 2 tablespoons olive oil
- ½ cup freshly grated Parmigiano-Reggiano
- ½ cup chopped fresh basil
  Freshly ground pepper

In a large slow cooker, combine the onion, salt, tomatoes, and water. Add the farro and stir. Cover and cook on high for 1½ to 2 hours, or until the farro is tender and the liquid is absorbed.

Stir in the oil, cheese, basil, and pepper to taste. Serve hot.

Risotto-Style Farro with Parmesan

Although made with farro, this recipe could just as well be made with Arborio rice, since the method is similar to the way you make risotto. Chopped onion, carrot, and celery are sautéed in butter until tender, then the farro and broth are added. Slow cooking allows the farro to absorb all the flavor and moisture as it becomes tender. As with risotto, the finishing touch is Parmigiano-Reggiano, which melts into the *farrotto*. The farro remains pleasantly chewy and is not as creamy as risotto.

SERVES 6

- 2 tablespoons unsalted butter
- 1 medium onion, finely chopped
- 1 medium carrot, finely chopped
- 1 medium celery rib, finely chopped
- 1½ cups whole-grain farro (see page 12), rinsed and picked over
- 2 cups Chicken Broth (page 46) or canned chicken or vegetable broth
- Salt and freshly ground pepper
- A large piece of Parmigiano-Reggiano or Grana Padano

In a medium skillet, melt the butter over medium heat. Add the onion, carrot, and celery and cook, stirring often, until the vegetables are tender, about 10 minutes. If they begin to turn brown, add a tablespoon or two of water and lower the heat.

Scrape the vegetables into a large slow cooker. Add the farro, broth, and salt and pepper to taste and stir well. Cook on high for 1½ to 2 hours, and then check to see that there is enough liquid in the pot. If necessary, stir in a little warm water. When the farro is tender yet still chewy and all the liquid has been absorbed, the farro is ready to serve. It keeps well on warm for up to 1 hour.

Just before serving, shave some of the cheese over the *farrotto* with a vegetable peeler and stir well.

Farro Salad

Farro is ideal for salads, since it combines well with other ingredients and keeps its chewy texture, never becoming mushy. It's a nice change from pasta or potato salads. Serve as a side dish with grilled fish steaks and a tossed salad or as a main dish with hard-cooked eggs and tuna packed in olive oil.

SERVES 8

- 2 cups whole-grain farro (see page 12)
- 4 cups water
- Salt
- 1/4 cup olive oil
- 2 tablespoons white wine vinegar
- 1 large garlic clove, minced
- Freshly ground pepper
- 1 cup diced roasted red bell pepper (jarred or homemade)
- 1 cup chopped flavorful black olives
- 1/2 cup chopped fresh parsley
- 4 anchovy fillets, finely chopped
- 2 tablespoons rinsed, drained, and chopped capers

In a slow cooker, combine the farro, water, and salt to taste. Cover and cook on high for 1½ hours, or until the farro is tender yet still chewy. If it seems dry, stir in a little warm water.

In a large bowl, whisk together the oil, vinegar, garlic, and pepper to taste. Drain the farro, if necessary. Stir the farro into the dressing. Let cool slightly.

Add the remaining ingredients and toss well. Serve warm or slightly chilled.

Seafood

Seafood

Braised Halibut Steaks

The pan juices from these fish steaks are full of flavor, so serve the fish with some rice or polenta.

SERVES 6

- 2 large tomatoes
- 3 tablespoons chopped fresh parsley
- 2 tablespoons fresh lemon juice
- 1/2 teaspoon dried oregano
- Salt and freshly ground pepper
- 2 tablespoons olive oil
- 2 tablespoons unsalted butter
- 2 garlic cloves, finely chopped
- 6 thick halibut steaks (2 pounds total) or other white fish steaks

Cut the tomatoes in half lengthwise and cut out the stem ends. Squeeze the tomatoes gently to extract the seeds. Chop the tomatoes and place them in a bowl; there should be about 2 cups. Add the parsley, lemon juice, oregano, and salt and pepper to taste.

In a small microwave-safe bowl, combine the oil, butter, and garlic. Cook on high for 1½ minutes, or until the garlic is fragrant. Stir the garlic mixture into the tomatoes.

Arrange the fish steaks in the slow cooker. Spoon on the tomato mixture.

Cover and cook on low for 1 to 1½ hours, or until the fish is just cooked through. Serve hot.

Salmon with Basil and Lemon

Salmon turns tender and moist in the slow cooker. The simple flavors of fresh basil and lemon complement the fillets, which can be served hot or cold. For a cool summer supper, serve it with Farro Salad (page 86) or Warm Lentil Salad (page 194).

SERVES 6

1 large red onion, thinly sliced

¼ cup dry white wine

1 cup water

1 thick salmon fillet (about 2 pounds), cut into 6 serving pieces

1 tablespoon olive oil

   Salt and freshly ground pepper

2 tablespoons fresh lemon juice

6 large fresh basil leaves, chopped

Scatter the onion slices in a large slow cooker. Add the wine and water.

Rinse the salmon pieces and pat dry. Rub the flesh side with the oil. Sprinkle with salt and pepper to taste. Place the salmon skin side down in the slow cooker. Sprinkle with the lemon juice and basil.

Cover and cook on low for 1 to 1½ hours, or until the salmon is cooked to taste. Serve hot or cold.

Tuna Meatballs in Tomato Sauce

I've never met a meatball I didn't like, and this one is no exception. The chopped fish is mixed with bread crumbs, cheese, and flavorings, shaped into balls, then simmered in a tasty tomato sauce. Tuna meatballs are perfect with pasta or on their own with a mixed salad.

Rather than buy expensive fresh tuna steaks for this recipe, I use the economical frozen fish steaks that many markets carry today. Once thawed, they are easy to chop in a food processor.

SERVES 8

MEATBALLS

¼ cup chopped pine nuts

2 pounds tuna or swordfish, thawed if frozen, cut into 1-inch chunks

2 large eggs, beaten

2 garlic cloves, finely chopped

¾ cup plain dry bread crumbs

½ cup freshly grated Pecorino Romano

⅓ cup dried currants or raisins

¼ cup chopped fresh parsley

2 tablespoons fresh lemon juice

1 tablespoon olive oil

1 teaspoon salt

Freshly ground pepper

SAUCE

2 medium onions, finely chopped

2 garlic cloves, finely chopped

3 tablespoons olive oil

1 28-ounce can tomato puree

1 teaspoon dried oregano

Pinch of salt

Chopped fresh basil or parsley

MAKE THE MEATBALLS: Toast the pine nuts in a small saucepan over medium heat, stirring occasionally, about 5 minutes. Set aside. In a food processor, pulse the fish chunks in small batches until coarsely chopped. Scrape the fish into a large bowl.

Add the remaining meatball ingredients, including the pine nuts, and blend well. With moistened hands, shape the mixture into 2½-inch balls.

MAKE THE SAUCE: In a large skillet, cook the onions and garlic in the oil over medium heat until tender and golden, about 10 minutes. Scrape the mixture into the slow cooker. Add the tomato puree, oregano, and salt and stir well.

Add the meatballs to the cooker, pressing them into the sauce. Cover and cook on low for 4 hours. Serve hot, sprinkled with the basil or parsley.

Cod with Potatoes

Mild-flavored fresh cod and potatoes get dressed in their Sunday best when they cook in a tasty sauce with tomato, onions, and green olives. To accompany the dish, serve a leafy green salad with a dressing of olive oil and fresh lemon juice.

SERVES 6

- 2 medium onions, thinly sliced
- 2 garlic cloves, finely chopped
- 1/4 cup olive oil
- 2 cups canned tomato puree
- 4 medium potatoes, thinly sliced
- 1/2 cup chopped celery
- 1 teaspoon dried oregano
- Salt and freshly ground pepper
- 1/2 cup pitted and chopped green olives
- 1 1/2 pounds cod, grouper, or other thick white fish fillets, cut into 6 serving pieces
- Chopped fresh parsley

In a large skillet, cook the onions and garlic in the oil over medium heat for 10 minutes, or until tender. Scrape them into a large slow cooker. Stir in the tomato puree, potatoes, celery, oregano, and salt and pepper to taste. Cover and cook on low for 2 hours, or until the potatoes are tender when pierced with a fork.

Stir in the olives. Pat the fish dry and place in the slow cooker. Baste the fish with the sauce. Cover and cook for 20 minutes, or until the fish is tender. Serve hot, sprinkled with the parsley.

Stuffed Calamari

Most familiar as deep-fried rings, calamari are also delicious left whole and stuffed with a tasty bread-crumb filling. Buy large calamari, which are easier to fill than small ones. Don't stuff them more than halfway, since they tend to shrink as they cook. They are good over polenta or spaghetti.

SERVES 4 TO 6

12 large (about 6 inches long) cleaned calamari with tentacles (1 1/2 pounds total)

1/3 cup fresh bread crumbs made from Italian or French bread

1/4 cup freshly grated Pecorino Romano

4 garlic cloves, finely chopped

1/4 cup finely chopped fresh parsley

2 tablespoons rinsed, drained, and chopped capers

Salt and freshly ground pepper

1/4 cup olive oil

1 28-ounce can tomato puree

Rinse the squid well inside and out and make sure the insides have been thoroughly cleaned.

Very finely chop the tentacles and scrape them into a bowl. Add the bread crumbs, cheese, half of the garlic, half of the parsley, the capers, and salt and pepper to taste. Add 2 tablespoons of the oil and stir until well blended.

Pat the calamari dry. With a small spoon, stuff each with a heaping teaspoon of the stuffing mixture. Don't add more or the filling will burst out as the calamari cook. With toothpicks, pin the calamari closed.

In a large skillet, heat the remaining 2 tablespoons oil over medium heat. Add the calamari and brown on one side. Turn the calamari, add the remaining garlic, and brown on the other side. Transfer the calamari to the slow cooker.

Add the tomato puree and salt and pepper to taste. Cover and cook on low for 2 hours, or until the squid are tender when pierced with a fork. Remove the toothpicks. Sprinkle the calamari with the remaining parsley and serve hot.

Clams Naples-Style

Fresh clams cooked in a garlic- and chile-spiked tomato sauce are a specialty of Naples. You'll find versions of this dish on the menu at many Italian restaurants in the United States, where it is often called Clams Posillipo, after the name of a little beach town that is a suburb of Naples. The recipe can also be made with mussels or a combination of clams and mussels.

SERVES 4

- 4 garlic cloves, very finely chopped
- 1/3 cup olive oil
- 1 cup dry white wine
- 2 28-ounce cans Italian peeled tomatoes with their juice, chopped
- 1 teaspoon dried oregano
- Pinch of salt
- 4 pounds littleneck, Manila, or other small clams (see headnote)
- Pinch of crushed red pepper
- 8 1/2-inch-thick slices Italian or French bread
- 1 whole garlic clove, peeled
- 2 tablespoons chopped parsley

In a small saucepan, cook the chopped garlic in the oil over medium heat until golden, about 2 minutes. Add the wine and bring it to a simmer. Pour the mixture into a large slow cooker. Add the tomatoes, oregano, and salt. Cover and cook on high for 3 hours.

Meanwhile, soak the clams in cold water to cover for 30 minutes, to remove any grit. Scrub them with a stiff brush. Discard any clams that do not close up tightly when tapped or any with cracked or broken shells.

When the sauce is ready, stir in the crushed red pepper and add the clams. Cook for 30 minutes more, or until the clams open. Discard any that do not open.

Just before serving, toast the bread and rub both sides with the whole garlic. Place the toast in serving bowls and top with the clams and sauce. Sprinkle with the parsley and serve hot.

Mussel, Saffron, and Fennel Stew

Fresh fennel has a mild licorice flavor that complements seafood. To trim fresh fennel, cut off a slice from the base and remove the green stems. Save the feathery leaves to use as a garnish. Remove any bruised spots.

SERVES 4

- 4 cups Chicken Broth (page 46) or canned chicken broth
- ½ teaspoon saffron threads
- 1 large onion, finely chopped
- 1 garlic clove, finely chopped
- ¼ cup olive oil
- 1 small fennel bulb, chopped (see headnote)
- 2 tomatoes, peeled, seeded, and chopped
- 4 small potatoes, diced
- 3 pounds mussels, soaked and scrubbed
- 2 tablespoons chopped fennel leaves or parsley

Pour 1 cup of the broth into a small bowl. Crumble the saffron threads into the bowl and set aside.

In a small skillet, cook the onion and garlic in the oil over medium heat for 10 minutes, or until tender. Scrape the mixture into the slow cooker. Add the chopped fennel, the remaining 3 cups broth, tomatoes, and potatoes. Cook on low for 2 hours, or until the vegetables are tender.

Add the mussels and saffron broth. Cover and cook for 30 minutes more, or until the mussels open. Discard any mussels that do not open.

Sprinkle with the fennel leaves or parsley and serve hot.

Tuscan Seafood Stew

Practically every region along Italy's long coastline has a special seafood stew, and each has a slight twist that makes it a little different from the others. Sometimes the stew is made with green peppers, others lack tomatoes, while some are made exclusively with fish and not shellfish. Needless to say, the inhabitants of each region insist theirs is the best!

This version with tomatoes, fish, and shellfish, but no green peppers, is my interpretation of one I had in Tuscany.

SERVES 6

  1 large onion, chopped
  2 large garlic cloves, finely chopped
  1/4 cup olive oil
  2/3 cup dry white wine
  2 1/2 pounds peeled, seeded, and chopped tomatoes, or one 28-ounce can Italian peeled tomatoes with their juice, chopped
  1 8-ounce bottle clam juice
  1/4 cup chopped fresh parsley, plus more for garnish
  1/2 pound cleaned calamari, cut into 1/2-inch rings
     Pinch of crushed red pepper
  1 pound firm-fleshed white fish fillets, such as monkfish or halibut
  1/2 pound medium shrimp, shelled and deveined
     Salt and freshly ground pepper
     Sliced Italian bread, toasted

In a saucepan, cook the onion and garlic in the oil over medium heat until the onion is tender and translucent, about 5 minutes. Add the wine and bring it to a simmer. Scrape the mixture into the slow cooker.

Add the tomatoes, clam juice, and parsley. Cover and cook on low for 3 hours. Add the squid and crushed red pepper and stir well. Add the fish and shrimp, submerging the pieces in the sauce. Cover and cook for 20 to 30 minutes, or until the fish is cooked and the sauce is simmering. Season with salt and pepper to taste.

Place a slice or two of toast in each bowl. Spoon on the fish and broth. Sprinkle with parsley and serve.

Seafood Couscous

Couscous topped with seafood is a revered specialty in and around Trapani, on the west coast of Sicily. Couscous is made by mixing coarsely ground wheat flour with water and rolling it into tiny beads. The partially precooked instant couscous is a good option.

For the fish, use whatever varieties of firm white fish look good in the market. Striped bass, monkfish, and halibut are good choices. Serve the couscous as they often do in Sicily, followed by a salad of sliced oranges, fennel, and red onion.

SERVES 6

- 2 medium onions, chopped
- 1/4 cup olive oil
- 4 garlic cloves, chopped
- 2 cups peeled, seeded, and chopped fresh or canned tomatoes
- 2 tablespoons tomato paste
- 1 bay leaf
- Pinch of ground cinnamon
- 3 cups clam juice, Chicken Broth (page 46) or canned chicken broth
- Salt

COUSCOUS

- 2 1/2 cups Chicken Broth (page 46) or canned chicken or fish broth
- 2 tablespoons olive oil
- Pinch of saffron, crumbled
- 1 1/2 cups instant couscous
- Salt

- Pinch of crushed red pepper
- 1 pound firm-fleshed white fish fillets or steaks, such as halibut, monkfish, or striped bass
- 1/2 pound large shrimp, shelled and deveined
- 1/2 pound sea scallops
- 2 tablespoons chopped fresh parsley

In a medium skillet, cook the onions in the oil over medium heat, stirring occasionally, until tender but not browned, about 10 minutes. If the onions start to color, add a tablespoon or two of water and lower the heat slightly. Stir in the garlic and cook for 2 minutes more.

Stir in the tomatoes, tomato paste, bay leaf, and cinnamon and bring to a simmer. Transfer the sauce to the slow cooker. Add the clam juice or broth and salt to taste. Cover and cook on low for 4 hours.

JUST BEFORE SERVING, MAKE THE COUSCOUS: In a medium saucepan, bring the broth, olive oil, and saffron to a simmer over medium heat. Stir in the couscous and salt to taste. Cover the pan and remove it from the heat. Let stand for 10 minutes.

Add the crushed red pepper and seafood to the slow cooker, spooning the sauce over the seafood. Cover and cook for 20 minutes, or until the seafood is just cooked through.

Fluff the couscous with a fork and spoon it onto a large, warm serving platter. Remove the seafood from the sauce and arrange it on top of the couscous. Spoon on enough of the sauce to moisten the couscous. Pour the rest of the sauce into a serving bowl. Sprinkle the seafood and couscous with the parsley. Serve hot, passing the additional sauce.

Eggs, Chicken, and Turkey

Eggs, Chicken, and Turkey

Sweet Red Pepper, Onion, and Potato Frittata

I make a frittata, an Italian-style omelet, when I want a terrific quick meal for breakfast, lunch, or dinner. Colorful and easy, a frittata is special enough to serve to guests, and leftovers make great sandwiches.

Typically, a frittata is made in a skillet, but it needs careful attention so that the eggs do not brown and become tough. In a slow cooker, a frittata takes only about an hour to cook, but once you turn it on, you can forget about it until you are ready to serve it. The gentle heat means a perfect golden frittata every time. While it cooks, you can make a salad and slice some crisp Italian bread to go with it.

SERVES 4 TO 6

- 2 tablespoons olive oil
- 2 large red bell peppers, seeded and sliced
- 1 medium onion, chopped
  Salt
  Butter
- 8 large eggs
- 2 tablespoons freshly grated Parmigiano-Reggiano
- 2 tablespoons chopped fresh parsley
  Freshly ground pepper
- 2 medium potatoes, boiled and sliced

In a large skillet, heat the oil over medium heat. Add the peppers and cook for 5 minutes. Add the onion and salt to taste. Cook, stirring often, until the peppers are tender and starting to brown, about 15 minutes. Let cool.

Generously butter the base and 2 inches up the sides of a large slow cooker.

In a large bowl, beat the eggs with the cheese, parsley, ½ teaspoon salt, and pepper to taste until well blended. Stir in the pepper mixture and potatoes. Pour into the slow cooker.

Cover and cook on high for 60 to 75 minutes, or until the frittata is just set when a knife is inserted in the center. Cut into wedges to serve.

Pasta Frittata

Concerned that a frittata is not substantial enough for dinner? This Neapolitan version will change your mind. Made with bits of chopped salami, peas, roasted peppers, and cheese entangled in spaghetti, it is held together by the beaten eggs. The pasta creates a pretty swirly pattern, while the vegetables and meat add lots of color and flavor. Cook the pasta from scratch or use leftovers with or without a sauce.

SERVES 6 TO 8

- 10 large eggs
- ½ cup freshly grated Parmigiano-Reggiano
- Salt and freshly ground pepper
- 1 cup thawed frozen peas
- ½ cup chopped roasted red bell pepper (jarred or homemade), drained and patted dry
- 4 ounces salami, prosciutto, or ham, chopped
- 8 ounces cooked spaghetti or other pasta (about 4 cups), with or without sauce
- Butter
- 4 ounces chopped mozzarella, fontina, or Asiago cheese

In a large bowl, whisk the eggs, Parmigiano-Reggiano, and salt and pepper to taste until blended. The cheese and meat are salty, so don't add too much salt. Stir in the peas, peppers, and meat. Add the pasta and toss well.

Generously butter the bottom and 2 inches up the sides of the slow cooker. Pour in the egg mixture. Scatter the chopped cheese on top, being careful not to touch the sides of the crock or the frittata will stick. Cover and cook on high for 60 to 75 minutes, or until a knife inserted in the center comes out clean.

Cut into wedges to serve.

Tomato, Ricotta, and Basil Frittata

This frittata is perfect for a light summer meal or a Sunday brunch. Serve as is or with juicy fried sausages and steamed asparagus.

SERVES 6

Butter

12 large eggs

1 cup freshly grated Parmigiano-Reggiano

1/4 cup chopped fresh basil

Salt and freshly ground pepper

1 cup halved cherry or grape tomatoes

8 ounces (1 cup) ricotta cheese

Generously butter the base and halfway up the sides of a slow cooker.

In a large bowl, whisk the eggs, cheese, basil, and salt and pepper to taste until well blended. Pour the mixture into the slow cooker. Scatter the tomatoes over the egg mixture. Dollop with tablespoons of the ricotta.

Cover and cook on high for 60 to 75 minutes, or until a knife inserted in the center comes out clean. Run a spatula around the inside of the slow cooker.

Cut into wedges to serve.

Chicken with Rosemary and Garlic

Here's a slow-cooked chicken seasoned with the classic flavorings for an Italian-style roast. Nothing could be easier, and the chicken turns out moist and juicy. I like to serve it with roasted potatoes as well as asparagus sprinkled with grated Parmigiano-Reggiano.

I also use this method when I need cooked chicken for salads (see page 129) or sandwiches.

SERVES 4 TO 6

1 4-pound chicken

   Salt and freshly ground pepper

3 large garlic cloves

2 3-inch fresh rosemary sprigs

1 tablespoon olive oil

Remove the neck and giblets from the chicken cavity and reserve them for another use. Trim away any excess fat.

Sprinkle the chicken inside and out with salt and pepper to taste. Put the garlic and rosemary inside the cavity and place the chicken in the slow cooker. Rub it all over with the oil. Cover and cook on low for 5 hours, or until the chicken is tender and the temperature in the thickest part of the thigh measures 165°F on an instant-read thermometer.

Remove the chicken from the slow cooker and cut into serving pieces. Skim the fat from the pan juices and discard. Drizzle the pan juices over the chicken. Serve hot.

Chicken Parmesan Heroes

The secret to a plump, juicy chicken breast is to not let the meat dry out with too high a heat or too long a cooking time. In this recipe, boneless, skinless chicken poaches gently in the simmering sauce on low heat, coming out fork-tender and as flavorful as can be. It's perfect for stuffing into crisp rolls for a fun (think messy) and easy hot-sandwich supper. Be sure to provide lots of napkins.

SERVES 6

- 4 cups Sweet Tomato Sauce (page 51) or Tomato and Red Wine Sauce (page 52)
- 6 boneless, skinless chicken breast halves
  Salt and freshly ground pepper
- 1/4 cup freshly grated Parmigiano-Reggiano
- 8 ounces mozzarella cheese, cut into 6 slices
- 6 fresh basil leaves
- 6 hero rolls

Pour the tomato sauce into the slow cooker. Pat the chicken pieces dry with paper towels and sprinkle with salt and pepper to taste. Place the pieces, overlapping slightly, in the sauce. Cover and cook on low for 3 hours.

Sprinkle the chicken with the Parmigiano-Reggiano and top each piece with a slice of mozzarella and a basil leaf. Cover and cook for 15 minutes more, or until the cheese is melted.

Cut the rolls partially open and fill each one with a cheese-covered chicken breast and sauce. Cut the sandwiches in half. Serve hot.

Sicilian-Style Orange Chicken

Oranges grow in abundance in Sicily, and cooks there use them not just for desserts but also in salads and sauces. In this recipe, orange juice, zest, garlic, and oregano combine with the chicken juices to make a delicious sweet and tart sauce.

Removing the skin before cooking the chicken is not essential, but it will be a healthier meal and will look better, since the skin does not brown in the slow cooker. To remove the skin, loosen it by inserting your fingers between the skin and the meat. Then pull the skin away from the meat with one hand, using a sharp paring or boning knife to cut it away from the meat wherever necessary.

SERVES 6

- 3½ **pounds bone-in chicken legs, thighs, and breasts (see headnote)**
- **Salt and freshly ground pepper**
- 4 **garlic cloves, minced**
- 1 **teaspoon dried oregano**
- 1 **cup orange juice**
- 2 **teaspoons cornstarch**
- 1 **teaspoon grated orange zest**
- 1 **tablespoon chopped fresh parsley**

Pat the chicken pieces dry with paper towels and arrange the pieces in a single layer in the slow cooker. Sprinkle with salt and pepper to taste, garlic, and oregano. Add ¾ cup of the orange juice. Cover and cook on low for 5 hours, or until the chicken is very tender.

Remove the chicken to a serving platter. Cover and keep warm. Pour the chicken juices into a small saucepan. Bring to a simmer. In a small bowl, stir together the remaining ¼ cup orange juice and the cornstarch until smooth. Add the cornstarch mixture to the saucepan and cook, stirring, until smooth and thickened, about 1 minute. Stir in the zest. Pour the sauce over the chicken. Sprinkle with the parsley and serve hot.

Lemon Chicken and Potatoes

Chicken roasted with potatoes, oregano, and lemon works well in the oven and is just as delicious—and even easier—in the slow cooker. The lemon slices become soft and mellow, sharing their flavor with the chicken and potatoes. Serve with some colorful vegetables, such as steamed carrots, green beans, or broccoli.

SERVES 4

- 4 medium potatoes, peeled and cut into wedges
- Salt and freshly ground pepper
- 3$\frac{1}{2}$ pounds bone-in chicken legs, thighs, and breasts, skin removed
- 2 tablespoons olive oil
- 2 medium onions, thinly sliced
- 2 garlic cloves, finely chopped
- 1 teaspoon dried oregano
- $\frac{1}{2}$ cup dry white wine
- 1 tablespoon fresh lemon juice
- 1 medium lemon, sliced and seeded

Scatter the potatoes in the slow cooker and sprinkle with salt and pepper to taste.

Pat the chicken pieces dry with paper towels and sprinkle with salt and pepper to taste.

In a large skillet, heat the oil over medium-high heat. Add the chicken pieces and cook until nicely browned on all sides, about 15 minutes. Place the chicken on top of the potatoes.

Add the onions to the skillet and cook until softened, about 5 minutes. Stir in the garlic and oregano and cook for 1 minute more. Add the wine and lemon juice and bring it to a simmer. Pour the mixture over the chicken and potatoes.

Cover and cook on high for 3 hours or on low for 5 hours. Tuck the lemon slices around the chicken pieces and cook for 1 hour more, or until the potatoes are tender and the chicken is cooked through. Serve hot.

Chicken with Vinegar and Garlic

Whole garlic cloves infuse this chicken with flavor, while a little vinegar gives it liveliness and sun-dried tomatoes add color. The only difficult thing about this easiest of recipes is waiting for it to be done! The juices are delicious, so serve this dish with some crisp bread to sop them up.

SERVES 6

- 3½ pounds bone-in chicken legs, thighs, and breasts, skin removed
- Salt and freshly ground pepper
- ¼ cup chopped sun-dried tomatoes (not oil-packed)
- 6 whole garlic cloves, unpeeled
- 3 3-inch fresh rosemary sprigs
- ½ cup dry red wine
- 2 tablespoons balsamic vinegar

Pat the chicken pieces dry with paper towels and sprinkle with salt and pepper to taste. Place the pieces in the slow cooker. Tuck the sun-dried tomatoes, garlic cloves, and rosemary around the chicken pieces. Pour on the wine and vinegar.

Cover and cook on low for 5 to 6 hours, or until the chicken is tender. Remove the chicken pieces to a platter. Discard the rosemary sprigs. Squeeze the garlic cloves to extract the garlic. Discard the skins. Mash the garlic into the sauce and pour it over the chicken. Serve hot.

Chicken with Peppers and Mushrooms

Every region of Italy seems to have its own version of chicken cacciatore, or hunter's style chicken, though no one is quite sure where the name came from. As the mushrooms, sweet bell peppers, and red wine simmer with the chicken in this southern Italian recipe, they create a delicious, full-flavored sauce. Serve over noodles or with good bread.

SERVES 4

- 1 4-pound chicken, cut into 8 pieces
  Salt and freshly ground pepper
- 2 tablespoons olive oil
- 2 large red bell peppers, seeded and cut into strips
- 12 ounces button mushrooms, halved
- 2 medium onions, finely chopped
- 1/2 teaspoon dried thyme
- 2 garlic cloves, finely chopped
- 2 tablespoons all-purpose flour
- 1 tablespoon tomato paste
- 3/4 cup dry red wine

Pat the chicken pieces dry with paper towels and sprinkle with salt and pepper to taste. Heat the oil in a large skillet over medium heat. Add the chicken pieces, in batches if necessary, skin side down. Cook until nicely browned. Carefully turn the pieces and brown the other side. Place the chicken in the slow cooker.

Pour off all but 2 tablespoons of the fat from the skillet. Turn the heat to medium-high. Add the peppers and mushrooms and cook, stirring frequently, until they begin to soften. Add the onions, thyme, and garlic and cook for 3 minutes more.

Sprinkle the flour over the vegetables. Cook, stirring constantly, for 1 to 2 minutes more. Add the tomato paste and wine and bring to a simmer, scraping the bottom of the pan with a spoon. Pour the contents of the pan over the chicken.

Cover and cook on high for 2½ hours or on low for 5 hours, or until the chicken is cooked through. Serve hot.

Chicken with Cherry Tomatoes, Capers, and Olives

A pinch of crushed red pepper imparts a hint of spiciness to the chicken, and olives and capers add rich and complex flavors. If you are making this dish the day before you plan to serve it, add the olives and capers when you reheat the chicken, to keep their flavors fresh and lively.

SERVES 6

- 4 pounds bone-in chicken legs, thighs, and breasts, skin removed
- 1 teaspoon dried oregano
  Salt and freshly ground pepper
- 1 pint cherry or grape tomatoes, halved
- 2 garlic cloves, chopped
- ¼ cup dry white wine
  Pinch of crushed red pepper
- ½ cup rinsed and drained imported black olives
- 2 tablespoons rinsed and drained capers

Pat the chicken pieces dry with paper towels and sprinkle with oregano and salt and pepper to taste. Place the pieces in the slow cooker. Add the tomatoes, garlic, and wine. Cover and cook on low for 5 hours, or until the chicken is cooked through.

Sprinkle with the crushed red pepper. Scatter the olives and capers around the chicken and cook for 15 to 30 minutes more. Serve hot.

Chicken with Pancetta, Peas, and Herbs

Although I usually opt for fresh vegetables, I always keep packages of frozen peas on hand. They are as good as, and often better than, the fresh peas I can buy, and they add great flavor and color to so many dishes. Teamed with pancetta, herbs, and wine, they make a great topping for chicken. Serve this with tender buttered egg noodles.

SERVES 6

    2 ounces pancetta (see page 13), chopped
    2 tablespoons olive oil
    1 large onion, chopped
    4 garlic cloves, finely chopped
    6 fresh sage leaves, chopped
    1 teaspoon chopped fresh rosemary
 3½ pounds bone-in chicken legs, thighs, and breasts, skin removed
    Salt and freshly ground pepper
    2 bay leaves
    ½ cup dry white wine, Chicken Broth (page 46), or canned chicken broth
    2 cups frozen peas, partially thawed

In a medium skillet, cook the pancetta in the oil over medium heat for 5 minutes. Add the onion, garlic, sage, and rosemary and cook for 10 minutes more, or until the onion is tender.

Pat the chicken pieces dry with paper towels and sprinkle with salt and pepper to taste. Place the pieces in the slow cooker. Scrape the pancetta mixture on top and add the bay leaves. Sprinkle with the wine or broth.

Cover and cook on low for 6 hours. Add the peas and baste with the liquid. Cover and cook for 20 minutes more, or until the chicken is cooked through. Serve hot.

Pesto Chicken

A blend of fresh basil, parsley, and garlic stuffed under the skin infuses the bird with flavor and helps keep it moist and juicy. The parsley keeps the pesto an appetizing bright green.

SERVES 4 TO 6

BASIL PESTO

3/4 cup fresh basil leaves

1/2 cup fresh parsley leaves

2 garlic cloves

Salt and freshly ground pepper

2 tablespoons olive oil

1 4-pound chicken

MAKE THE PESTO: In a food processor, chop the basil, parsley, and garlic until fine. Add salt and pepper to taste. Blend in the oil.

MAKE THE CHICKEN: Remove the neck and giblets from the chicken cavity and reserve them for another use. Trim away any excess fat.

Sprinkle the chicken inside and out with salt and pepper to taste. Carefully lift the chicken skin covering the legs and breasts. With your fingers, spread the pesto between the surface of the meat and the skin. Place the chicken in the slow cooker.

Cover and cook on low for 5 hours, or until the chicken is tender and cooked through. Serve hot.

Braised Chicken and Vegetables with Green Sauce

Here's a perfect Sunday supper: chicken cooked on a bed of vegetables with a classic *salsa verde*, or green sauce, made from parsley, garlic, anchovies, and olive oil. Any leftover sauce keeps well for several days in the refrigerator and is excellent on grilled fish or meat or on sliced tomatoes.

SERVES 4

- 4 large red potatoes, thickly sliced
- 2 large carrots, thickly sliced
- 2 cups 1-inch-cubed butternut squash
- 1 large onion, sliced
- Salt and freshly ground pepper
- 1 4-pound chicken
- ½ lemon
- 4 garlic cloves, peeled
- 1 3-inch fresh rosemary sprig

  GREEN SAUCE

- 2 ½-inch-thick slices Italian or French bread, crusts removed
- 2 cups packed fresh parsley
- 1 garlic clove
- 4 anchovy fillets
- ¾ cup olive oil
- 2 tablespoons fresh lemon juice
- Salt and freshly ground pepper

MAKE THE CHICKEN AND VEGETABLES: Scatter the potatoes, carrots, squash, and onion in the slow cooker. Sprinkle with salt and pepper to taste.

Remove the neck and giblets from the chicken cavity and reserve them for another use. Trim away any excess fat.

Sprinkle the chicken inside and out with salt and pepper to taste. Squeeze the lemon half over the chicken. Place the lemon half, garlic cloves, and rosemary in the cavity. Place the chicken on top of the vegetables.

Cover and cook on low for 5 hours, or until the chicken is cooked through and the vegetables are tender.

MEANWHILE, MAKE THE GREEN SAUCE: Soak the bread in warm water for 5 minutes. Drain and squeeze out most of the liquid.

In a food processor, combine the parsley, garlic, and anchovies and process until finely chopped. Add the soaked bread. With the machine running, drizzle in the oil and lemon juice. Add salt and pepper to taste. (You will have 1 cup.)

Cut the chicken into serving pieces and serve with the vegetables. Pass the green sauce at the table.

Chicken Salad with Summer Vegetables

Fresh tomatoes, cucumber, and red onion combine with a slow-cooked chicken in this easy summer salad. For variety, try this salad with other vegetables, such as shredded carrots, green onions, or fresh cooked corn kernels. If you want to make it with leftover chicken, the recipe can easily be halved. For the best flavor, serve the salad immediately after combining the ingredients.

SERVES 6

- 1/2 cup olive oil
- 3 tablespoons red wine vinegar
- Pinch of ground marjoram
- Salt and freshly ground pepper
- Chicken with Rosemary and Garlic (page 113)
- 2 large ripe tomatoes, chopped
- 1 small cucumber, peeled and chopped
- 1/2 small red onion, thinly sliced
- 1/2 cup chopped fresh parsley
- Lettuce leaves

In a large bowl, whisk together the oil, vinegar, marjoram, and salt and pepper to taste.

Discard the chicken skin and bones and cut the meat into bite-size pieces. Add the chicken to the dressing and toss well. Add the tomatoes, cucumber, onion, and parsley and toss again. Taste for seasoning.

Arrange the lettuce leaves on a platter. Spoon the chicken and vegetables on top and serve.

Rolled Stuffed Turkey Breast

Hot or cold, this tender, boneless turkey breast stuffed with prosciutto, garlic, and rosemary is delicious. It also makes a great sandwich, layered with arugula and mayonnaise.

SERVES 6

- ½ boneless turkey breast (about 2½ pounds)
- 2 garlic cloves, finely chopped
- 1 tablespoon chopped fresh rosemary
- Salt and freshly ground pepper
- 2 ounces sliced prosciutto
- 2 medium carrots, cut into chunks
- 2 medium celery ribs, cut into chunks
- 1 medium onion, thickly sliced
- ½ cup Chicken Broth (page 46) or canned chicken broth

With a small, sharp knife, remove the turkey skin in one piece and set it aside. Starting at one long side, cut the turkey breast almost in half lengthwise, stopping just short of the other side. Open the turkey breast like a book. Flatten the meat with a mallet to an even thickness.

Sprinkle the turkey with half of the garlic, half of the rosemary, and salt and pepper to taste. Lay the prosciutto over the meat. Roll up the turkey. Sprinkle with the remaining garlic and rosemary, and salt and pepper to taste. Spread the turkey skin over the rolled-up meat. Tie the roll at 2-inch intervals with kitchen twine.

Scatter the carrots, celery, and onion in the slow cooker. Pour in the broth. Place the turkey roll on top. Cook on high for 2 to 2½ hours, or until the meat measures 155°F on an instant-read thermometer.

Remove the turkey from the cooker and cover it to keep warm. Let stand for 15 minutes before slicing.

Strain the juices into a small saucepan. Bring the liquid to a simmer and cook until slightly reduced.

Remove and discard the turkey skin and the twine. Slice the turkey and arrange the slices, overlapping slightly, on a platter. Spoon the sauce over the slices and serve warm or cold.

Turkey Tonnato

Veal tonnato, a classic Italian first course, consists of thinly sliced poached veal covered with a sauce made with canned tuna. It may sound unlikely, but it is very tasty and works beautifully with turkey breast instead of veal. In summer, I serve this as a main course with crisp arugula leaves and sliced tomatoes. It's good for a party, because you can make and assemble the entire dish ahead of time.

Leftover turkey makes great cold sandwiches, and the sauce can be served over hard-cooked eggs and boiled potatoes or as a dip for raw vegetables.

SERVES 8

½ boneless turkey breast (about 2½ pounds), rolled and tied
Salt and freshly ground pepper
2 medium carrots, sliced
2 medium celery ribs, sliced
1 medium onion, sliced
1 cup Chicken Broth (page 46), canned chicken broth, or water

SAUCE

1 6½-ounce can tuna packed in olive oil
4 anchovy fillets
½ cup mayonnaise
2 tablespoons rinsed and drained capers
1 small garlic clove
½ teaspoon grated lemon zest
1½–2 tablespoons fresh lemon juice, plus more if needed

GARNISH

1 tablespoon rinsed and drained capers
5 or 6 lemon slices
1 tablespoon chopped fresh parsley

MAKE THE TURKEY: Sprinkle the turkey with salt and pepper to taste. Scatter the vegetables in the slow cooker. Add the broth or water and place the turkey on top. Cover and cook on high for 2½ to 3 hours, or until an instant-read thermometer placed in the thickest part of the meat registers 155°F. Remove the turkey from the cooker, cover it to keep warm, and let stand for 10 minutes.

MEANWHILE, MAKE THE SAUCE: Combine all the sauce ingredients in a food processor or blender. Process until smooth, scraping the sides. Taste and add more lemon juice, if needed. The sauce should just coat the back of a spoon. If it is too thick, strain some of the cooking liquid in to thin it.

Spread some of the sauce on a platter. Slice the turkey and arrange the slices on top, overlapping slightly. Spoon on the remaining sauce. Garnish with the capers, lemon slices, and parsley. If not serving immediately, cover with plastic wrap, refrigerate for up to 3 hours, and serve cold.

Turkey and Spinach Loaf

Adding spinach and mushrooms to the ground turkey gives this meat loaf extra flavor and ensures that it turns out moist and juicy. Serve it with potatoes mashed with a little olive oil.

SERVES 8

1½ pounds fresh spinach, trimmed, or one 10-ounce package frozen spinach

¼ cup water (if using fresh spinach)

Salt

3 slices Italian bread

1½ pounds ground turkey

1 cup chopped mushrooms

4 ounces pancetta (see page 13), chopped

1 garlic clove, finely chopped

2 large eggs

1 cup freshly grated Parmigiano-Reggiano

¼ teaspoon ground nutmeg

Freshly ground pepper

1 cup peeled, seeded, and chopped fresh or canned tomatoes

½ cup Chicken Broth (page 46) or canned chicken broth

Fold a 2-foot length of aluminum foil in half lengthwise. Place the foil in the slow cooker, pressing it against the bottom and up the sides.

In a large pot, combine the fresh spinach, water, and salt to taste. Cover and cook until tender. If using frozen spinach, cook it according to the package directions. Drain well and let cool. Squeeze the spinach to extract the liquid. Chop the spinach finely and place it in a large bowl.

Soak the bread in a little water until soft. Crumble the moistened bread into the bowl. (You should have about ½ cup.) Add the turkey, mushrooms, pancetta, garlic, eggs, cheese, nutmeg, and salt and pepper to taste. Mix well.

With moistened hands, shape the turkey mixture into a loaf and place it in the slow cooker. Add the tomatoes and broth. Cover and cook on low for 3 hours, or until the loaf is cooked through.

Carefully lift the meat loaf out of the pan using the ends of the foil as handles. Slide the meat loaf onto a serving platter. Slice and serve hot.

Sweet Peppers Stuffed with Turkey, Prosciutto, and Cheese

Sweet bell peppers are a colorful and tasty container for ground-turkey filling. If you can find them, use a combination of red, yellow, and orange peppers. Serve them with hot cooked orzo or another small pasta to soak up the sauce.

SERVES 6

- 2 tablespoons olive oil
- 1 medium onion, finely chopped
- 1 medium carrot, finely chopped
- 1 medium celery rib, finely chopped
- 1 garlic clove, finely chopped
- 1 pound lean ground turkey
  Salt and freshly ground pepper
- 1/2 cup dry red wine
- 2 ounces prosciutto or ham, finely chopped
- 3/4 cup freshly grated Parmigiano-Reggiano
- 2 tablespoons chopped fresh parsley
- 1 cup plain dry bread crumbs
- 6 large red and orange or yellow bell peppers
- 2 cups canned tomato puree

In a large skillet, heat the oil over medium heat. Add the onion, carrot, celery, and garlic. Cook, stirring frequently, until the vegetables are golden.

Add the turkey and salt and pepper to taste. Cook, stirring often to break up the lumps, until the meat is no longer pink. Add the wine and bring it to a simmer. Cook until the wine has evaporated. Remove the skillet from the heat and let the turkey cool slightly. Stir in the prosciutto or ham, cheese, parsley, and bread crumbs.

Cut the tops off the peppers and remove the stems and seeds. Loosely stuff the peppers with the turkey mixture. Replace the tops.

Pour the tomato puree into the slow cooker. Arrange the peppers side by side in a single layer in the cooker. Cover and cook on high for 3 hours or on low for 5 hours, or until the peppers are tender when pierced with a knife. Serve hot.

Beef, Veal, Pork, and Lamb

Beef, Veal, Pork, and Lamb

Beef in Barolo

Hearty Barolo is the wine of choice for this pot roast in Piedmont, in northern Italy, but any good dry red wine can be substituted. The sauce is enhanced with vegetables and a hint of ground cloves. Serve with potato gnocchi or Creamy Polenta with Gorgonzola and Mascarpone (page 81).

SERVES 6

- 1/3 cup all-purpose flour
- Salt and freshly ground pepper
- 1 3-pound boneless beef chuck or bottom round roast
- 3 tablespoons olive oil
- 2 ounces pancetta (see page 13), chopped
- 1 medium onion, chopped
- 2 garlic cloves, finely chopped
- 1 cup dry red wine, such as Barolo
- 2 cups peeled, seeded, and chopped fresh or canned tomatoes
- 1 cup Meat Broth (page 47) or canned beef broth
- 2 medium carrots, sliced
- 1 medium celery rib, sliced
- 1 bay leaf
- Pinch of ground cloves

Combine the flour with salt and pepper to taste. Spread the mixture on a piece of wax paper and roll the meat in the flour.

In a large, heavy skillet, heat the oil over medium-high heat. Add the beef and brown it on all sides, about 15 minutes. Place the meat in a large slow cooker. Add the pancetta and onion to the skillet. Reduce the heat to medium and cook for 10 minutes, stirring occasionally, until the onion is tender. Stir in the garlic. Add the wine and bring it to a simmer, scraping the bottom of the pan.

Pour the mixture over the beef. Add the tomatoes and broth. Scatter the carrots, celery, bay leaf, and ground cloves around the meat. Cover and cook on low for 6 hours, or until the meat is tender when pierced with a fork.

Transfer the meat to a platter. Remove the bay leaf from the sauce. Slice the meat and spoon on the sauce.

Peppery Beef Stew

Traditionally, the brick makers of Impruneta, a town outside of Florence in Tuscany, cooked *peposo* in handmade clay pots and baked it slowly in the kilns they used to make bricks, so I knew it would be perfect for the slow cooker.

The black peppercorns soften as they cook and add a bite to the sauce. For a seriously peppery flavor, increase the amount of peppercorns or ground pepper. And if you want a real taste of Tuscany, serve this stew with Tuscan-Style Beans (page 193).

SERVES 6

- ½ cup all-purpose flour
- Salt
- 3 pounds boneless beef chuck, cut into 2-inch chunks
- 3 tablespoons olive oil
- 1 cup dry red wine, such as Chianti
- 2 cups canned tomato puree
- 2 garlic cloves, chopped, plus 6 whole garlic cloves, peeled
- 1 tablespoon whole black peppercorns, or to taste
- ½ teaspoon freshly ground pepper, or to taste

On a piece of wax paper, stir together the flour and salt to taste. Toss the beef with the flour and shake off any excess. In a large, heavy skillet, heat the oil over medium-high heat. Add the meat in batches, without crowding the pan. Brown the beef well on all sides. With a slotted spoon, transfer the beef to a large slow cooker.

Add the wine to the skillet and bring it to a simmer, scraping the bottom of the pan. Add the tomato puree, garlic, peppercorns, and ground pepper. Cook for 10 minutes, or until slightly thickened. Pour the mixture into the slow cooker. Cover and cook on low for 6 to 8 hours, or until the beef is very tender. Taste for seasoning before serving.

Beef Goulash

The cooking of northern Italy's Trentino-Alto Adige region often has more in common with neighboring Austria than with the rest of Italy, as you'll see with this delicious stew flavored with paprika. Some of the best paprika, which is made from ground chile peppers, comes from Hungary. Sweet paprika, not hot, is recommended here.

SERVES 6 TO 8

- 3 tablespoons lard, drippings, or vegetable oil
- 3½ pounds boneless beef chuck, cut into 2-inch cubes
- Salt and freshly ground pepper
- 4 medium onions, sliced
- 2 garlic cloves, finely chopped
- 1 cup dry red wine
- 2 tablespoons tomato paste
- 1 bay leaf
- ¼ cup sweet paprika
- 1 tablespoon chopped fresh marjoram leaves
- 1 teaspoon ground cumin
- 1 2-inch strip lemon zest
- Juice of ½ lemon

Heat the lard, drippings, or oil in a large, heavy skillet over medium-high heat. Pat the meat dry and add only as many pieces to the pan as will fit comfortably without crowding. Cook until nicely browned on all sides. Transfer the meat to a large slow cooker and brown the remaining meat. Sprinkle the meat with salt and pepper to taste.

When all the beef has been browned, reduce the heat to medium and add the onions to the skillet. Cook, stirring occasionally, until lightly browned. Stir in the garlic. Add the wine and tomato paste and bring to a simmer. Pour the mixture into the slow cooker.

Stir in the bay leaf, paprika, marjoram, cumin, and lemon zest. Add enough water to barely cover the meat. Cover and cook on low for 6 hours, or until the beef is very tender when pierced with a fork.

Stir in the lemon juice. Remove the bay leaf and lemon zest. Serve hot.

Spiced Beef Stew

Tired of the same old beef stew? This version has a touch of cinnamon, cloves, and nutmeg, giving it a subtly different flavor. In Trentino-Alto Adige, in northern Italy, venison is often substituted for the beef. Serve with mashed potatoes, buttered polenta, or potato gnocchi.

SERVES 6

- 1 tablespoon unsalted butter
- 1 tablespoon olive oil
- 3 pounds boneless beef chuck, cut into 2-inch pieces
- Salt and freshly ground pepper
- 2 medium onions, chopped
- 1 cup dry red wine
- 1 cup Meat Broth (page 47) or canned beef broth
- 3 tablespoons tomato paste
- 2 tablespoons all-purpose flour
- $1/8$ teaspoon ground cinnamon
- $1/8$ teaspoon ground cloves
- $1/8$ teaspoon freshly grated nutmeg

In a large, heavy skillet over medium-high heat, melt the butter with the oil. Pat the meat dry and add only as many pieces to the pan as will fit comfortably without crowding. Cook until nicely browned on all sides. Transfer the meat to a large slow cooker and brown the remaining meat. Sprinkle it with salt and pepper to taste.

Reduce the heat to medium, add the onions to the pan, and cook, stirring often, until tender and lightly browned. Add the wine and stir well, scraping the bottom of the pan. Bring the liquid to a simmer and cook for 1 minute. Pour the mixture into the cooker.

Stir together the broth and tomato paste. Add the flour and spices and stir until completely smooth. Pour the mixture into the slow cooker.

Cover and cook on low for 6 hours, or until the meat is very tender. Serve hot.

Braised Beef with Anchovies and Rosemary

Italian cooks often add anchovies to stews and braised meats. They melt and disappear into the sauce, adding a savory flavor that is very different from the aggressive effect of anchovies on a pizza or salad.

SERVES 6

- 2 tablespoons olive oil
- 4 pounds beef shin or 3 pounds boneless chuck, cut into 2-inch cubes
- 2 ounces pancetta (see page 13), chopped
- Salt and freshly ground pepper
- 2 large garlic cloves, finely chopped
- 6 anchovy fillets
- 1 cup dry white wine
- 1 3-inch fresh rosemary sprig

In a large, heavy skillet, heat the oil over medium-high heat. Pat the beef dry. Add only as much of the beef and pancetta to the pan as will fit comfortably without crowding. Cook until nicely browned on all sides. Transfer the meat to a large slow cooker and brown the remaining meat. Sprinkle the meat with salt and pepper to taste.

Spoon off the excess fat from the pan and reduce the heat to medium. Add the garlic and anchovies and cook, stirring, for 2 minutes, or until the anchovies dissolve. Add the wine and bring it to a simmer, scraping the bottom of the pan. Pour the liquid into the slow cooker. Add the rosemary.

Cover and cook on low for 6 hours, or until the meat is very tender. Discard the rosemary and serve hot.

Braciole in Tomato Sauce

Large, thin slices of beef rolled around a filling are called *braciole* (bra-*cho*-lay) in Italian. Vary the filling by stuffing them with a sprinkling of pine nuts and raisins or with slices of prosciutto and cheese.

SERVES 6 TO 8

- 2 ½-inch-thick beef round steaks (each about 1 pound)
- Salt and freshly ground pepper
- ½ cup freshly grated Pecorino Romano
- 3 tablespoons chopped fresh parsley
- 4 garlic cloves, finely chopped
- 2 tablespoons olive oil
- 1 large onion, chopped
- 1 28-ounce can tomato puree
- 6 fresh basil leaves, torn into bits

Place each steak between two sheets of plastic wrap. Gently pound the steaks with a mallet or the bottom of a small pan to a ⅛-inch thickness. Cut each steak in half. Sprinkle the meat with salt and pepper to taste, then with the cheese, parsley, and garlic. Roll up each piece of meat. With kitchen twine, tie each roll up like a roast.

In a large, heavy skillet, heat the oil over medium-high heat. Add the meat rolls and cook until browned on one side. Turn the rolls and scatter the onion around the meat. Cook until the meat is browned on all sides and the onion is tender. Transfer the rolls and onion to a large slow cooker and add the tomato puree and basil. Cover and cook on low for 4 hours, or until the meat is tender.

Transfer the meat to a cutting board. Remove the twine and cut the meat into thick slices. Spoon on the sauce. Serve hot.

Beef Shanks with Red Wine and Tomatoes

With long, slow cooking, thick slices of beef shank become infused with flavor and so tender you can cut them with a spoon. There's no need to brown the beef first. Have plenty of warm, toasted Italian bread ready to sop up the juices and eat with the garlic and the marrow from the bones.

SERVES 8

About 20 whole garlic cloves (1 large head), peeled
2   cups dry red wine
1   14-ounce can Italian peeled tomatoes with their juice, chopped
1   4-inch fresh rosemary sprig or 1 tablespoon dried
3   pounds bone-in beef shanks, about 2 inches thick, trimmed
Salt and freshly ground pepper
Thick-sliced Italian bread

Scatter the garlic cloves in the slow cooker. Add the wine, tomatoes, and rosemary. Place the beef in the cooker and sprinkle with salt to taste and plenty of pepper. Cover and cook on low for 6 to 8 hours, or until the meat is tender and falling off the bone.

Skim off the excess fat and taste for seasoning.

Toast the bread and place 1 or 2 slices in each serving dish. Break the meat up with a spoon and ladle some of the meat, garlic, and pan juices over the bread. Serve with the marrow bones.

Balsamic-Glazed Short Ribs

Sweet and mellow, balsamic vinegar adds a rich dark color and delectable flavor to falling-off-the-bone-tender short ribs.

SERVES 6

- 1 tablespoon olive oil
- 4–5 pounds bone-in beef short ribs, well trimmed
- Salt and freshly ground pepper
- 2 large garlic cloves, finely chopped
- ½ cup dry red wine
- ⅓ cup balsamic vinegar
- 1 3-inch fresh rosemary sprig

Heat the oil in a large, heavy skillet over medium-high heat. Pat the meat dry and add only as many pieces to the pan as will fit comfortably without crowding. Cook until nicely browned on all sides. Transfer the meat to a large slow cooker and brown the remaining meat. Sprinkle the ribs with salt and pepper to taste.

Discard all but 1 tablespoon of the fat and reduce the heat to medium. Add the garlic and cook for 1 minute. Add the wine and vinegar and bring to a simmer, scraping the bottom of the pan. Pour the liquid over the ribs and add the rosemary.

Cover and cook on low for 8 hours, or until the ribs are very tender. Remove the ribs from the slow cooker and discard the rosemary sprig and any loose bones. Cover the ribs and keep warm.

Skim the fat off the liquid. Pour the remaining sauce into a saucepan and cook over medium-high heat until reduced and slightly thickened. Spoon the sauce over the ribs and serve hot.

Roman Oxtail Stew

Many avid meat lovers have never tried oxtails. Too bad, because these chunky sections of beef tail have an amazing beefy flavor and are perfect for soups and slow-cooked stews like this one from Rome. I'm not sure who came up with the idea of adding celery, chocolate, pine nuts, and raisins to the pot, but the combination makes a brilliant balance of sweet and savory.

Serve with rigatoni or mashed potatoes and a green salad.

SERVES 6

- ¼ cup olive oil
- 4 pounds oxtails, about 1½ inches thick
- 1 large onion, chopped
- 2 garlic cloves, chopped
- 1 cup dry red wine
- 1 28-ounce can Italian peeled tomatoes with their juice
- ¼ teaspoon ground cloves
-   Salt and freshly ground pepper
- 6 medium celery ribs, sliced
- 1 tablespoon chopped bittersweet chocolate
- 2 tablespoons pine nuts
- 2 tablespoons raisins

In a large, heavy skillet, heat the oil over medium-high heat. Add the oxtails, in batches if necessary, and brown nicely on all sides. Transfer the oxtails to the slow cooker. Pour off all but 2 tablespoons of the fat and lower the heat to medium.

Add the onion to the skillet and cook until lightly browned, about 10 minutes. Stir in the garlic and cook for 30 seconds. Add the wine and scrape the bottom of the pan. Stir in the tomatoes, cloves, and salt and pepper to taste. Bring the liquid to a simmer, then pour over the oxtails.

Cover and cook on low for 6 hours, or until the meat is very tender and coming away from the bones.

Meanwhile, bring a large saucepan of water to a boil. Add the celery and cook for 1 minute. Drain well.

Turn the slow cooker to high. Stir in the chocolate. Add the celery, pine nuts, and raisins. Cook for 30 minutes, or until the flavors blend. Serve hot.

"Big Meatball" Meat Loaf

Instead of making small meatballs, I shape the ingredients into a loaf, known as a *polpettone* in Italian.

SERVES 8

2 pounds ground beef chuck or round

3 large eggs, beaten

2 garlic cloves, minced

1 cup freshly grated Pecorino Romano

¹/₂ cup plain dry bread crumbs

¹/₄ cup chopped fresh parsley

1¹/₂ teaspoons salt

Freshly ground pepper

2 cups meatless tomato sauce, such as Tomato and Red Wine Sauce (page 52) or Sweet Tomato Sauce (page 51)

Fold a 2-foot length of aluminum foil in half lengthwise. Place the foil in a large slow cooker, pressing it against the bottom and up the sides.

In a large bowl, mix together all the ingredients except the tomato sauce. Shape the mixture into a loaf. Carefully place it in the slow cooker on top of the foil. Pour the tomato sauce over the top.

Cover and cook on high for 4 hours, or until an instant-read thermometer reads 165° to 170°F.

Carefully lift the meat loaf out of the pan using the ends of the foil as handles. Slide the meat loaf onto a serving platter. Cut into slices and serve.

Sausage and Beef Meat Loaf

A combination of beef, pork sausage, and chopped vegetables makes this meat loaf especially tasty. I like to serve it with roasted potato wedges and broccoli sautéed with garlic.

SERVES 6

- 2 tablespoons olive oil
- 2 medium onions, chopped
- 1 cup chopped carrots
- 1 cup chopped celery
- 2 $3/4$-inch-thick slices Italian bread
- $1/2$ cup water
- $1 1/4$ pounds ground beef chuck
- $1/2$ pound sweet Italian sausage, casings removed
- 2 large eggs
- 2 garlic cloves, finely chopped
- $1/4$ cup chopped fresh parsley
- $1 1/2$ teaspoons salt
- $1/4$ teaspoon freshly ground pepper
- 2 tablespoons all-purpose flour
- $3/4$ cup Meat Broth (page 47) or canned beef broth
- $3/4$ cup dry white wine

Fold a 2-foot length of aluminum foil in half lengthwise. Place the foil in a large slow cooker, pressing it against the bottom and up the sides.

Heat the oil in a large skillet over medium heat and cook half the onions with the carrots and celery until tender and golden, about 10 minutes. Scrape the vegetables into the slow cooker.

In a small bowl, drizzle the bread with the water. Let stand for 5 minutes, or until the water is absorbed. Squeeze the bread dry and crumble it into a large bowl. There should be about ¾ cup. Add the remaining onion, the beef, sausage, eggs, garlic, parsley, salt, and pepper. Mix well with your hands. Shape the meat into a loaf and carefully transfer it to the slow cooker.

Stir together the flour, broth, and wine until smooth. Pour the liquid around the meat loaf. Cover and cook on low for 4 to 5 hours, or until the temperature reads 165° to 170° F on an instant-read thermometer.

Let stand for 30 minutes. Carefully lift the foil, allowing the liquid to drain back into the slow cooker. Slide the meat loaf onto a platter. Cut into slices, spoon the sauce over the top, and serve.

Springtime Veal Stew

Spring vegetables added toward the end of the cooking time bring color and fresh flavor to this stew. Vary the vegetables as you like. Other good choices are precooked or thawed frozen artichoke wedges, green beans, pearl onions, and sautéed mushrooms.

If you are making this stew ahead of time, add the vegetables when you reheat it.

SERVES 6

- 3 large carrots, cut into ¼-inch-thick slices
- 2 medium onions, chopped
- 3 tablespoons olive oil
- 1 garlic clove, finely chopped
- 2 teaspoons chopped fresh rosemary
- 2 pounds veal shoulder or chuck, trimmed and cut into 2-inch pieces
- 2 cups Chicken Broth (page 46) or canned chicken broth
- 2 tablespoons tomato paste
  Salt and freshly ground pepper
- 4 cups water
- 1 cup fresh asparagus, cut into 1-inch pieces
- 1 cup thawed frozen green peas or baby lima beans (see headnote)

Scatter the carrot slices in a large slow cooker.

In a large skillet, cook the onions in the oil over medium heat until softened, about 10 minutes. Stir in the garlic and rosemary. Add the veal and cook, stirring occasionally, until the meat is no longer pink. Scrape the veal mixture into the slow cooker.

Return the skillet to the heat and add the broth and tomato paste. Cook, stirring, until the liquid comes to a simmer, then pour into the slow cooker. Add a pinch of salt and pepper to taste. Cover and cook on low for 4 hours, or until the veal is tender when pierced with a fork.

Bring the water to a boil in a medium saucepan. Add the asparagus and salt to taste. Simmer for 3 to 5 minutes, depending on the thickness, until crisp-tender. Drain well.

Add the asparagus and the peas or beans to the slow cooker. Cover and cook for 30 minutes more, or until heated through. Serve hot.

Osso Buco with Red Wine

The name *osso buco* translates as "bone with a hole," an accurate description of the look of these meaty cross sections of veal shank. When buying the veal shanks, look for thick slices with more meat than bone.

This is a perfect dish for an important meal.

SERVES 6

- 6 1½-inch-thick slices veal shank
- ¼ cup all-purpose flour
-     Salt and freshly ground pepper
- 2 tablespoons unsalted butter
- 1 tablespoon olive oil
- 2 medium carrots, chopped
- 1 medium onion, chopped
- 1 medium celery rib, chopped
- 1 cup dry red wine
- 1 cup peeled, seeded, and chopped fresh or canned tomatoes
- 1 cup Meat Broth (page 47), Chicken Broth (page 46), or canned beef or chicken broth
- 2 teaspoons chopped fresh thyme or ½ teaspoon dried

To help hold the shape of the meat as it cooks, tie a piece of kitchen twine around the circumference of each shank.

On a piece of wax paper, stir together the flour and salt and pepper to taste. In a large, heavy skillet, melt the butter with the oil over medium heat. Dip the cut sides of each piece of meat in the flour mixture and place it in the skillet, in batches if necessary. Cook, turning the meat once, until nicely browned, about 10 minutes on each side. Transfer the browned meat to the slow cooker.

Add the chopped vegetables to the skillet. Cook, stirring occasionally, until golden brown, about 15 minutes. Add the wine to the skillet and cook, scraping the bottom of the pan, until the liquid comes to a boil. Stir in the tomatoes, broth, and thyme.

Pour the sauce over the veal. Cover and cook on low for 4 to 5 hours, or until the meat is very tender when pierced with a fork.

Remove the twine and serve hot.

Milk-Braised Pork Loin

When I first heard about this dish, I thought the combination of milk and pork sounded strange. But since I've never met a pork dish I didn't like, I had to try it. Trust me! You will love this one as much as I do. The milk bubbles away and leaves just a small amount of thick, creamy sauce speckled with little bits of carrot, onion, and celery surrounding the tender, flavorful pork. It makes a fine Sunday dinner.

SERVES 6 TO 8

- 3 pounds boneless pork loin, rolled and tied
- Salt and freshly ground pepper
- 2 tablespoons unsalted butter
- 1 tablespoon olive oil
- 2 medium carrots, finely chopped
- 1 medium onion, finely chopped
- 1 medium celery rib, finely chopped
- 2 cups whole milk

Pat the meat dry with paper towels. Sprinkle it with salt and pepper to taste.

In a large, heavy skillet over medium-high heat, melt the butter with the oil. Brown the meat on one side. Turn it over and scatter the vegetables around the meat. Cook until the vegetables are golden.

Transfer the meat to the slow cooker. Add the milk to the skillet with the vegetables and bring it to a simmer. Pour the contents of the skillet over the meat. Cover and cook on low for 3 to 4 hours, or until an instant-read thermometer inserted in the center of the meat measures 160°F.

If the sauce is too thin, pour it into a saucepan and reduce it over medium heat. Remove the twine from the meat. Slice the meat and arrange the slices, overlapping slightly, on a platter. Spoon the sauce down the center and serve hot.

Pork Chops with Fennel Seeds

Fennel seeds add a flavor twist to these simple pork chops, which go well with Chickpea Stew (page 195).

SERVES 6

- 6 bone-in pork rib chops (about 3½ pounds total)
  Salt and freshly ground pepper
- 2 tablespoons olive oil
- 2 large onions, thinly sliced
- ½ cup dry white wine
- 1 tablespoon fennel seeds
- 1 cup Meat Broth (page 47) or canned beef broth

Pat the pork chops dry with paper towels and sprinkle them on both sides with salt and pepper to taste.

In a large, heavy skillet, heat the oil over medium-high heat. Add as many of the chops as will fit in the pan without touching. Cook, turning the chops occasionally, until nicely browned on all sides. Place the browned chops in the slow cooker. Brown the remaining pork chops.

Add the onions to the skillet, reduce the heat to medium, and cook for about 10 minutes, or until very tender but not browned. If the onion starts to color, add a little water to prevent them from burning. Stir in the wine and fennel seeds and bring it to a simmer. Add the broth and scrape the bottom of the pan until boiling. Pour the mixture over the chops.

Cover and cook on low heat for 6 to 8 hours, or until the meat is very tender and falling away from the bone. Serve hot.

Pork Stew Agrodolce

Raisins and vinegar give a sweet-and-sour (*agrodolce*) tang to this tasty pork stew. Serve it with sautéed sweet peppers and Basic Polenta (page 77).

SERVES 6 TO 8

- 3 pounds boneless pork shoulder, cut into 2-inch pieces
- Salt and freshly ground pepper
- 3 tablespoons olive oil
- 3 large onions, chopped
- 2 large celery ribs, chopped
- 1 cup dry white wine
- 3 tablespoons balsamic vinegar
- 3 large carrots, cut into 1-inch chunks
- 1/2 cup golden raisins

Pat the pork dry with paper towels. Sprinkle the meat with salt and pepper to taste.

In a large, heavy skillet, heat the oil over medium-high heat. Add the pork, without crowding the pan. Brown the meat on all sides and transfer it to the slow cooker.

When all the meat has been browned, reduce the heat to medium. Add the onions and celery to the skillet and cook, stirring frequently, until golden.

Add the wine and vinegar and bring it to a simmer. Transfer the onion mixture to the slow cooker. Add the carrots and raisins. Cover and cook on low for 6 hours, or until the pork is tender. Serve hot.

Country-Style Pork Ribs with Tomato and Peppers

Meaty country-style pork ribs are a great choice for the slow cooker. They turn out moist and tender and never lack for flavor. Here they are cooked in a spicy sauce made with red bell peppers and tomato. Serve it over polenta or mashed potatoes with zesty broccoli rabe cooked with garlic.

SERVES 6

- 4 pounds country-style pork ribs
- Salt and freshly ground pepper
- 2 tablespoons olive oil
- 2 medium onions, chopped
- 2 large garlic cloves, chopped
- 1/2 cup dry white wine
- 2 tablespoons tomato paste
- 1 cup canned tomato puree
- 1 teaspoon dried oregano
- 4 medium red bell peppers, seeded and cut into 1/2-inch slices

Pat the ribs dry with paper towels and sprinkle them with salt and pepper to taste. In a large skillet, heat the oil over medium heat. Add as many of the ribs as will fit in the pan without touching. Cook the meat, turning it occasionally, until nicely browned on all sides. Place the browned ribs in the slow cooker and brown the remaining ribs.

Add the onions and garlic to the skillet and cook for 5 minutes, or until softened. Stir in the wine and tomato paste and cook, scraping the bottom of the pan, until the liquid begins to simmer. Stir in the tomato puree, oregano, and salt and pepper to taste. Remove from the heat.

Scatter the peppers over the pork in the slow cooker. Pour on the sauce. Cover and cook on low for 6 hours, or until the meat is tender and coming away from the bones. Discard any loose bones and skim off the fat. Serve hot.

Spareribs with Spicy Sausages

On a cold, rainy December day in Rome, we trudged past the steamy windows of an old trattoria. We could barely see the interior, but it seemed warm and cozy, just what we were craving. Inside, we were quickly shown to a table, where the waitress recited the simple menu. I chose spareribs prepared in a rich tomato sauce with mildly spiced sausage. It was served over soft, creamy yellow polenta. When I make my version at home, I sometimes toss the meat and sauce with chunky pasta or serve it over tender cooked cannellini beans.

SERVES 6

- 2 tablespoons olive oil
- 3 pounds meaty spareribs, cut into individual ribs
- 3 hot Italian sausages, cut into 1-inch chunks
- 1 medium onion, chopped
- 1 medium carrot, chopped
- 1 medium celery rib, chopped
- 1 large garlic clove, finely chopped
- 1 28-ounce can tomato puree
- Salt and freshly ground pepper

In a large skillet, heat the oil over medium heat. Add the meats in batches and brown on all sides. Place the browned meats in the slow cooker. Add the chopped vegetables to the pan and cook, stirring, until tender and golden. Stir in the tomato puree and a pinch of salt and pepper, scraping the bottom of the pan. Bring the sauce to a simmer. Pour it into the cooker.

Cover and cook on low for 8 hours, or until the meat is falling away from the bones. Serve hot.

Lamb Stew with Sun-Dried Tomatoes

Lamb shoulder stays moist even when cooked for a long time, so it is the perfect choice for this recipe. This is good with boiled new potatoes and buttered asparagus.

SERVES 6

- 3 pounds boneless lamb shoulder, trimmed of fat and cut into 2-inch pieces
- 3 tablespoons olive oil
- Salt and freshly ground pepper
- 2 medium carrots, chopped
- 1 medium onion, chopped
- 1 garlic clove, finely chopped
- 1 tablespoon finely chopped fresh rosemary
- 1/2 cup dry white wine
- 2 tablespoons tomato paste
- 1/2 cup sun-dried tomatoes (not oil-packed), cut into narrow strips
- 2 cups Meat Broth (page 47) or canned beef broth
- 1 tablespoon chopped fresh parsley

Pat the meat dry with paper towels. Heat the oil in a large skillet over medium-high heat. Add the lamb a few pieces at a time and brown well on all sides. Transfer the browned meat to a slow cooker and brown the remaining lamb. Sprinkle it with salt and pepper to taste.

Turn the heat to medium. Add the carrots and onion to the pan. Cook, stirring occasionally, until tender and golden. Add the garlic, rosemary, wine, and tomato paste and bring it to a simmer. Scrape the mixture into the slow cooker.

Add the sun-dried tomatoes and broth. Cover and cook on low for 6 hours, or until the lamb is tender. Serve hot, sprinkled with the parsley.

Lamb Shanks with White Beans and Gremolata

Lamb and beans are made for each other. In this hearty stew, a sprinkle of gremolata—a tasty blend of lemon, parsley, and garlic—adds a lively touch to the finished dish. All you need is a green vegetable, such as broccoli, to complete the meal.

SERVES 4

- 1 medium onion, chopped
- 1 medium carrot, chopped
- 1 medium celery rib, chopped
- 4 garlic cloves, chopped
- 1 3-inch fresh rosemary sprig
- 4 small lamb shanks (about 1 pound each)
  Salt and freshly ground pepper
- 1 cup Meat Broth (page 47) or canned beef broth
- 1 cup dry red wine
- 2 tablespoons tomato paste
- 4 cups cooked white beans (Basic Beans, page 191) or canned beans, drained
- 1/4 cup chopped fresh parsley
- 2 garlic cloves, minced
- 1 teaspoon grated lemon zest

Scatter the vegetables, chopped garlic, and rosemary in the slow cooker.

Trim the shanks, pat them dry with paper towels, and sprinkle with salt and pepper to taste. Arrange the shanks in a single layer on top of the vegetables.

Stir together the broth, wine, and tomato paste. Pour the mixture over the lamb. Cover and cook on low for 8 hours, or until the lamb is very tender and coming away from the bone.

Remove the shanks from the cooker and place on a serving platter. Cover and keep warm.

Skim the fat off the surface of the liquid in the cooker. Turn the heat to high. Stir in the beans and cook until heated through.

Meanwhile, chop together the parsley, minced garlic, and lemon zest. Stir half the mixture into the beans. Pour the beans over the lamb. Sprinkle with the remaining gremolata and serve hot.

Lamb Shanks with Sweet Peppers and Olives

These lamb shanks simmer in broth and wine until the meat nearly falls off the bone. Meanwhile, the sweet peppers are cooked separately so that they keep their shape and texture. Along with a handful of black olives, the peppers add color, flavor, and texture to the sauce. Served with Tuscan-Style Beans (page 193), the shanks are my idea of a perfect meal.

SERVES 4

- 2 tablespoons olive oil
- 4 small lamb shanks (about 1 pound each), well trimmed
  Salt and freshly ground pepper
- 1/2 cup dry white wine
- 1 garlic clove
- 1 2-inch fresh rosemary sprig or 1/2 teaspoon dried
- 1 cup Meat Broth (page 47) or canned beef broth
- 1 tablespoon unsalted butter
- 2 medium red or yellow bell peppers, seeded and cut into 1/2-inch strips
- 1/2 cup pitted and chopped imported black olives
- 2 tablespoons chopped fresh parsley

In a large skillet, heat the oil over medium heat. Pat the lamb shanks dry with paper towels and add them to the skillet. Brown well on all sides. Sprinkle with salt and pepper to taste and place the shanks in the slow cooker.

Pour off the fat from the skillet. Add the wine, garlic, and rosemary and bring it to a simmer, scraping the bottom of the pan. Pour the wine mixture over the shanks in the cooker. Add the broth. Cover and cook on high for 6 hours, or until the shanks are tender and the meat is falling away from the bone.

Remove the shanks from the cooker, place on a serving platter, and keep warm. Strain the liquid and skim off the fat. Place the liquid in a small saucepan and bring to a boil. Cook until slightly reduced and thickened.

Meanwhile, melt the butter in a small skillet. Add the peppers, 2 tablespoons of the reduced cooking liquid, and salt and pepper to taste. Cover and cook for 10 minutes, or until the peppers are almost tender. Stir in the olives, parsley, and the remaining cooking liquid. Bring to a simmer and pour the sauce over the lamb. Serve hot.

Vegetables and Dried Legumes

Vegetables and Dried Legumes

Artichokes with Pancetta and Onion

Artichokes are typically trimmed and cooked whole, but in this recipe, the tough leaves are trimmed off and the hearts are cut into wedges. They cook slowly with tasty bits of pancetta (Italian bacon) and onion until they are buttery soft and tender. They are a nice side dish with roast lamb or fish, and I have even served them over pasta with great success.

SERVES 6

- 1 lemon, halved
- 6 medium artichokes
- 2 ounces pancetta (see page 13), chopped
- 2 tablespoons olive oil
- 1 large onion, finely chopped
- 1/2 cup dry white wine
- 1 teaspoon salt
- Freshly ground pepper

Fill a large bowl with cold water. Squeeze the lemon juice into the water and drop in the lemon halves.

With a serrated knife or very sharp chef's knife, trim off the top ¾ to 1 inch of the artichoke leaves. With scissors, trim the pointed tops off the remaining leaves. Bend back and snap off the small tough leaves around the base and one or two rows of darker green leaves all around the artichokes. With a vegetable peeler or sharp paring knife, remove the tough outer skin of the stems. Cut each artichoke into 8 wedges. Trim away the fuzzy choke. Drop the trimmed wedges into the bowl of lemon water.

In a medium skillet, cook the pancetta in the oil over medium heat until lightly golden, about 5 minutes. Add the onion and cook until tender and golden, about 10 minutes. Drain the artichokes and place them in the slow cooker. Add the onion mixture, wine, salt, and pepper to taste. Stir well.

Cover and cook on high for 2 hours, or until artichokes are tender. Serve hot.

Mom's Stuffed Artichokes

My mom made artichokes like this all the time. The filling is an Italian classic: a mixture of bread crumbs, fresh parsley, salty grated cheese, chopped garlic, and olive oil. The stuffing is tucked into the center of each trimmed artichoke and between the leaves. Simmered in the slow cooker, the artichokes become nice and tender. Serve as a first course or after the main course, in place of a salad. (See the photo on page 178.)

SERVES 6

- 1 lemon, halved
- 6 medium artichokes
- 6 tablespoons freshly grated Pecorino Romano or Parmigiano-Reggiano
- 1 garlic clove, very finely chopped
- ¼ cup chopped fresh parsley
- ⅔ cup plain dry bread crumbs
- Salt and freshly ground pepper
- ¼ cup olive oil

Fill a large bowl with cold water. Squeeze the lemon juice into the water and drop in the lemon halves.

With a serrated knife or very sharp chef's knife, trim off the top ¾ to 1 inch of the artichoke leaves. With scissors, trim the pointed tops off the remaining leaves. Bend back and snap off the small tough leaves around the base and one or two rows of darker green leaves all around the artichokes. Cut off the stems so that the artichokes can stand upright. With a vegetable peeler or sharp paring knife, remove the tough outer skin of the stems. Add the stems to the bowl of lemon water.

To remove the chokes, gently spread the leaves of the artichokes open. Use a small knife with a rounded tip to scrape out the fuzzy leaves in the center. Place the artichokes in the lemon water.

With a large chef's knife, finely chop the artichoke stems. Mix the stems with the cheese, garlic, parsley, bread crumbs, and salt and pepper to taste. Stir in 2 tablespoons of the oil until the crumbs are evenly moistened.

Drain the artichokes and pat them dry with paper towels. Holding an artichoke upright in one hand, lightly stuff the center with some of the bread-crumb mixture and add a little stuffing between the leaves. Do not pack the stuffing in tightly or it will become too heavy. Repeat with the remaining artichokes.

Pour 1 inch of water into the slow cooker. Add salt to taste. Stand the stuffed artichokes upright in the cooker side by side. Drizzle with the remaining 2 tablespoons oil.

Cover and cook on high for 3½ to 4 hours, or until the artichokes are completely tender when pierced through the base with a sharp knife and a leaf pulls out easily. Serve warm or at room temperature.

Romano Beans with Prosciutto

If Italian flat beans are not available, make this with green beans, which will require a shorter cooking time.

SERVES 4 TO 6

- 1 large onion, chopped
- 2 tablespoons olive oil
- 2 ounces sliced prosciutto, cut into $1/2$-inch squares
- $1^1/_2$ pounds Italian flat beans (see headnote), trimmed and cut into 1-inch pieces
- 1 cup chopped canned tomatoes with their juice
- 1 tablespoon chopped fresh marjoram, thyme, or basil
- Salt and freshly ground pepper

In a small skillet, cook the onion in the oil over medium heat until tender but not browned, about 10 minutes. Stir in the prosciutto and cook for 2 minutes more.

Place the beans in the slow cooker. Add the onion mixture, tomatoes, fresh herb, and salt and pepper to taste. Cover and cook on high for 1½ hours. Stir the beans and cook for 30 minutes more, or until the beans are very tender. Serve hot.

Beet Salad with Orange Dressing

Beets with their bright green tops still attached will be freshest and have the best flavor. Cook the tops like spinach and serve them tossed with garlic sautéed in olive oil.

As an alternative to the orange dressing, toss the cooked beets with a dressing made from oil, wine vinegar, garlic, and chopped mint, or serve them hot with butter and chopped fresh chives.

SERVES 6

- **2** bunches medium beets (6–8)

DRESSING

- **1–2** navel oranges
- **2–3** tablespoons balsamic vinegar
- **2** tablespoons olive oil
- Salt and freshly ground pepper

Trim off the stems about ½ inch above the beets. Reserve the leaves for another recipe (see headnote). Do not trim the roots from the beets. Scrub the beets and wrap each one separately in foil. Place the beets in the slow cooker. Cover and cook on high for 3½ to 4 hours, or until a small, sharp knife can easily pierce them. Let the beets cool slightly.

MAKE THE DRESSING: Grate about ½ teaspoon orange zest into a medium bowl. Halve the oranges and squeeze until you have ⅓ cup juice. Add the juice to the bowl along with 2 tablespoons of the vinegar, the oil, and salt and pepper to taste. Whisk until blended.

Unwrap the beets and slip off the skins. Trim off the roots and the base of the stems. Cut the beets into bite-size pieces. Add the beets to the bowl and toss well. Taste for seasoning, adding more vinegar, if needed. Serve warm or slightly chilled.

Cauliflower with Prosciutto and Olives

Serve this cauliflower tossed with hot cooked pasta as a main course or with roast chicken as a side dish.

SERVES 6

- 1 large cauliflower (about 1½ pounds), trimmed and cut into 1-inch florets
- ¼ cup olive oil
  Salt
- ½ cup Chicken Broth (page 46) or canned chicken broth
- ½ cup coarsely chopped pitted olives of your choice
- 3 ounces sliced prosciutto, cut into narrow strips
  Freshly ground pepper
- 2 tablespoons chopped fresh parsley

Place the cauliflower in the slow cooker. Add the oil and a pinch of salt and toss well. Add the broth. Cover and cook on high for 1½ hours, or until almost tender.

Add the olives and prosciutto and toss well. Cook for 30 to 45 minutes more. Season to taste with salt and pepper. Sprinkle with the parsley. Serve hot.

Sicilian Cauliflower with Raisins and Pine Nuts

If you are having a hard time convincing your family to try cauliflower, serve them this recipe. It is easy to love! The vegetable is smothered in a tasty tomato sauce with sweet bits of raisins and pine nuts. Sometimes I mash the cooked cauliflower and serve this over pasta.

SERVES 8

- 1 medium onion, chopped
- 3 tablespoons olive oil
- 1½ cups peeled, seeded, and chopped fresh or canned tomatoes
- ½ cup dry white wine or tomato juice
- 1 large cauliflower (about 1½ pounds), trimmed and cut into florets
- ¼ cup dark raisins
- ¼ cup pine nuts
- Salt and freshly ground pepper
- 2 tablespoons finely chopped fresh parsley

In a small skillet, cook the onion in the oil over medium heat until very tender. Stir in the tomatoes and wine or juice and bring to a simmer. Cook for 1 minute.

In a slow cooker, combine the cauliflower, raisins, pine nuts, tomato mixture, and salt and pepper to taste. Cover and cook on high for 2 hours, or until the cauliflower is tender when pierced with a knife. Sprinkle with the parsley and serve hot.

Spinach Parmesan Sformato

Sformato is the Italian word for food that is shaped in a mold and served un-molded. Think of this as a fallen soufflé or a molded omelet. Serve it for brunch with a tomato salad and bread or as an elegant side dish with a roast. For a more elaborate presentation, surround the *sformato* with sautéed mushrooms or peas.

Spinach is delicious prepared this way, or try another vegetable, such as broccoli, asparagus, peas, or green beans. You will need 1 cup of pureed cooked vegetables.

SERVES 4

- 1 pound spinach (see headnote), cooked, cooled, and squeezed in a towel to extract excess liquid
- 6 large eggs
- 3/4 cup freshly grated Parmigiano-Reggiano
- Pinch of freshly grated nutmeg
- Salt and freshly ground pepper
- 1 tablespoon melted unsalted butter

Place the spinach in a food processor and blend until smooth. Add the eggs, cheese, nutmeg, and salt and pepper to taste. Blend until smooth.

Brush a 6-cup soufflé dish or a heatproof bowl with the butter. Pour in the spinach mixture. Place it in the slow cooker, cover, and cook on high for 1½ hours, or until the mixture is just set when a knife is inserted in the center.

Carefully remove the *sformato* from the slow cooker. Run a small knife around the inside of the dish and invert it onto a serving plate. Serve hot.

Butternut Squash and Potatoes with Rosemary

Here's another dish that I used to bake in the oven but now prefer to make in my slow cooker because it is so easy. The vegetables steam with garlic and rosemary in a little water and olive oil. The flavors of the squash and potatoes blend, while their texture becomes soft and creamy. Serve it as is, or add a few chopped black olives and a sprinkle of chopped fresh parsley. Acorn, hubbard, and other firm winter squashes are great cooked this way.

SERVES 6

- 1½ pounds potatoes, peeled and cut into ½-inch wedges (about 4 cups)
- 1½ pounds butternut squash (see headnote), peeled and cut into 1-inch cubes (about 4 cups)
- 6 garlic cloves
  Salt and freshly ground pepper
- ¼ cup olive oil
- ¼ cup water
- 1 2-inch fresh rosemary sprig

Place the potatoes, squash, and garlic in the slow cooker. Sprinkle with salt and pepper to taste. Drizzle with the oil and toss well. Add the water and tuck the rosemary sprig among the vegetables.

Cover and cook on high until the vegetables are tender when pierced with a knife, about 3 hours. Serve hot.

Summer Squash
with Tomatoes and Onion

Use whatever varieties of summer squash you can find to make this colorful stew. It is good hot or at room temperature with barbecued chicken. Any leftovers are great folded into an omelet.

SERVES 6 TO 8

2 pounds summer squash, such as zucchini, yellow, or pattypan, trimmed and cut into $1/2$-inch pieces

2 medium red or yellow bell peppers, cut into bite-size pieces

1 large onion, chopped

1 cup halved grape or cherry tomatoes

2 tablespoons chopped fresh marjoram or basil

3 tablespoons olive oil

Salt and freshly ground pepper to taste

In a slow cooker, combine all the ingredients and toss well. Cover and cook on high for 2 hours, or until the vegetables are tender but not mushy. Serve hot or at room temperature.

Zucchini and Potatoes

I sometimes add halved cherry tomatoes to this simple combination of vegetables. If you have some fresh basil, tear up a few leaves and stir them in just before serving.

SERVES 6

- 4 medium zucchini (about 1¼ pounds), cut into ½-inch-thick slices
- 3 medium potatoes (about 1 pound), cut into ¼-inch-thick slices
- 2 tablespoons olive oil
- 1 large onion, chopped
- ½ teaspoon dried oregano
  - Salt and freshly ground pepper to taste
- ¼ cup water
- 2 tablespoons freshly grated Parmigiano-Reggiano

In a slow cooker, combine all the ingredients except the cheese. Stir well. Cover and cook on high for 1½ to 2 hours, or until the potatoes are tender. Sprinkle with the cheese just before serving.

Braised Potatoes with Tomatoes and Onions

Italians call these potatoes *alla pizzaiola*, because the tomato, oregano, and cheese flavors are reminiscent of pizza. Serve them with pork chops or steak.

SERVES 6

- 2 large onions, thinly sliced
- 2 tablespoons olive oil
- 1½ cups peeled, seeded, and chopped fresh or canned tomatoes
- 1 teaspoon dried oregano
- 2 pounds potatoes, such as Yukon Gold, peeled and cut into bite-size pieces
- Salt and freshly ground pepper
- ½ cup freshly grated Parmigiano-Reggiano

In a medium skillet, cook the onions in the oil over medium heat until tender and golden, about 8 minutes. Stir in the tomatoes and oregano.

In the slow cooker, combine the onion mixture, potatoes, and salt and pepper to taste. Stir well. Sprinkle with the cheese. Cover and cook on low for 3 hours. Serve hot.

Basic Beans

This is my favorite way to cook dried beans. Not only do they taste better and have less sodium than canned, but they also cost less. For convenience, I like to make a big batch and store them in small containers in the freezer, then use them for soups, stews, salads, dips, and pasta sauces.

Other bean varieties can be prepared this way, but you may have to adjust the cooking time.

SERVES 6

1 pound dried beans, such as cannellini, Great Northern, or cranberry beans, rinsed and picked over

6 cups water

1 bay leaf or fresh rosemary sprig (optional)

Salt

Place the beans in a slow cooker with the water and herb, if using. Cover and cook on low for 8 to 10 hours, or until tender. Add salt to taste and let stand for about 10 minutes. If you used the herb, remove it before serving.

Beans with Pancetta, Tomatoes, and Sage

Think of this recipe as the Italian version of pork and beans. It is a perfect complement to grilled chicken, sausages, or pork.

SERVES 8

- 1 pound dried cannellini or Great Northern beans, rinsed and picked over
- 2 fresh sage sprigs
- 3 large garlic cloves
- 2 ounces pancetta (see page 13) or thick-sliced bacon, chopped
- 3 large tomatoes, peeled, seeded, and chopped, or 2 cups diced canned tomatoes
- 6 cups water
- Salt

In a large slow cooker, combine the beans with all the remaining ingredients except the salt. Cover and cook on low for 10 to 12 hours, or until the beans are soft.

Add salt to taste and let stand for 10 minutes before serving. Serve warm.

Tuscan-Style Beans

Until I tried making beans in a slow cooker, I was never able to duplicate the creamy texture of those I enjoyed in Italy. Now they turn out that way every time. Serve these as a side dish with a juicy steak or roast, use them for soups, or top them with chunks of good tuna canned in olive oil and thin slices of red onion for a tasty and easy appetizer.

Soaking is not essential, but I find that this step helps the beans cook more evenly and makes them more digestible. If you don't soak them, just put the rinsed and sorted beans in the cooker with the water and seasonings and cook them a little longer.

Remember that cooking times will vary according to how fresh the beans are, the kind of cooker you are using, and whether they have been soaked or not.

If you have a prosciutto or other ham bone or a piece of the rind, add it to the pot for more flavor. (See the photo on page 172.)

SERVES 6

- 1 pound dried Great Northern or cannellini beans, rinsed and picked over
- 4 garlic cloves
- 6–8 fresh sage leaves or one 3-inch fresh rosemary sprig
  Salt
  Extra-virgin olive oil
  Freshly ground pepper

Place the beans in a large bowl with cold water to cover by several inches. Let stand at room temperature for 6 hours or in the refrigerator overnight.

Drain the beans and place them in a large slow cooker. Add water to cover the beans by 1 inch. Add the garlic and herb. Cover and cook the beans on low for 6 hours, or until the beans are tender and creamy. Check occasionally to see that the beans are covered with water. If necessary, add a little more.

Add salt to taste and let stand for 10 minutes. To serve, drain the beans, drizzle with the oil, and sprinkle with pepper to taste.

Warm Lentil Salad

Tiny brown lentils are used to make a salad like this in Umbria. I like it with grilled salmon or roast pork.

SERVES 8 TO 10

> 1 pound brown lentils, rinsed and picked over
>
> 6 cups water
>
> Salt
>
> 2 tablespoons olive oil
>
> 4 ounces thick-sliced pancetta (see page 13), cut into $1/2$-inch pieces
>
> 1 cup chopped shallots
>
> 2 medium celery ribs, chopped
>
> 1 large carrot, chopped
>
> 1 large garlic clove, finely chopped
>
> 2 tablespoons red wine vinegar
>
> $1/4$ cup chopped fresh parsley
>
> Freshly ground pepper

Put the lentils in a slow cooker and add the water. Cover and cook on low for 4 hours, or until tender. Add salt to taste. Let stand for 10 minutes.

Meanwhile, in a large skillet, heat the oil over medium heat and cook the pancetta until lightly browned, about 10 minutes. Transfer the pancetta to a plate with a slotted spoon.

Add the shallots, celery, carrot, and garlic to the skillet. Cook, stirring often, until the vegetables are golden and tender, about 15 minutes. Stir in the vinegar and cook for 1 minute more.

Drain the lentils and add them to the skillet. Add the pancetta and parsley. Stir well. Season with salt and pepper to taste. Serve warm.

Chickpea Stew

Canned chickpeas, potatoes, tomatoes, and onion flavored with rosemary cook into a chunky vegetarian main-dish stew. This also makes a great side dish for pork or lamb.

SERVES 6

- 3 16-ounce cans chickpeas, rinsed and drained
- 5 medium carrots, sliced
- 2 medium potatoes, peeled and chopped
- 1 cup peeled, seeded, and chopped fresh or canned tomatoes with their juice
- 1 medium onion, chopped
- 2 teaspoons chopped fresh rosemary
- ½ cup Chicken Broth (page 46), canned chicken or vegetable broth, or water
- 2 tablespoons olive oil
-    Salt and freshly ground pepper

Combine all the ingredients in a large slow cooker. Cover and cook on low for 6 to 8 hours, or until the vegetables are tender. Serve hot or at room temperature.

Desserts

Desserts

Orange-Glazed Apples

I like these apples for breakfast with a scoop of thick Greek-style yogurt.

SERVES 6

- $1/2$ cup walnuts, coarsely chopped
- $1/2$ cup orange marmalade
- 6 Granny Smith or Golden Delicious apples, cored
- $1/2$ cup dry white wine
- 1 3-inch strip orange zest
- $1/2$ cup sugar

In a small bowl, mix together the nuts and 2 tablespoons of the marmalade. Stuff the mixture into the apples. Place the apples in the slow cooker. Pour the wine around the apples. Add the zest.

Spoon the remaining 6 tablespoons marmalade on top of the apples. Sprinkle with the sugar.

Cover and cook on low for 3 to 4 hours, or until the apples are tender when pierced with a knife. Remove the apples from the cooker and pour the juices over them. Cover and refrigerate. Serve cold.

Apricot Baked Apples

For a real treat, melt some vanilla ice cream and serve as a sauce over these apples.

SERVES 6

1 cup chopped dried apricots

½ cup golden raisins

6 Golden Delicious apples, cored

½ cup sugar

½ cup dry white wine or apple juice

1 2-inch strip lemon zest

In a small bowl, mix together the apricots and raisins. Stuff the apples with the mixture. Place the apples in the slow cooker. Sprinkle the tops with the sugar. Pour the wine or juice around the apples. Place the lemon zest in the liquid.

Cover and cook on low for 3 to 4 hours, or until the apples are tender when pierced with a knife. Serve hot or cold with the cooking juices.

Pears in Marsala

A rich, brown glaze coats these succulent pears. Creamy mascarpone is the ideal accompaniment, or try them with a mild blue cheese, such as Gorgonzola dolce.

SERVES 6 TO 8

- 1/2 cup packed brown sugar
- 3/4 cup Marsala (see page 12)
- 1/2 cup orange juice
- 1 cinnamon stick
- 6–8 firm ripe pears, such as Bosc or Anjou

In a slow cooker, stir together the sugar, wine, orange juice, and cinnamon stick. Place the pears upright in the cooker and spoon some of the liquid over them. Cover and cook on high for 2 hours or on low for 4 hours, or until the pears are tender when pierced with a knife.

Uncover and let the pears cool in the cooker, basting them from time to time. Carefully transfer the pears to a serving dish. Discard the cinnamon stick. Pour the juices over the pears and chill until serving time.

Cherry-Spiced Pears

There's no need to peel or core these pears, which become fully tender through-out in the slow cooker. Red wine and dried cherries turn them a beautiful ruby red. They are great for a party or on a buffet.

SERVES 6 TO 8

- ⅔ cup sugar
- 1 cup dry red wine
- Grated zest and juice of 1 lemon
- 1 teaspoon whole black peppercorns
- 1 teaspoon allspice berries
- 1 cinnamon stick
- 6–8 firm, ripe pears, such as Bosc or Anjou
- ½ cup dried cherries, preferably the tart Montmorency variety
- Whipped cream (optional)

In a slow cooker, combine the sugar, wine, lemon zest and juice, and spices. Stand the pears upright in the cooker and spoon some of the liquid over them.

Cover and cook on high for 2 hours or on low for 4 hours, or until the pears are tender when pierced with a sharp knife.

Carefully transfer the pears to a serving dish. Strain the juices into a small saucepan. Add the cherries. Cook on high until the juices are thickened and re-duced. Pour the cherries and syrup over the pears. Cover and chill.

Serve plain or with whipped cream.

Dried Fruit Compote

These fruits are delightful with yogurt or sour cream or when spooned over a slice of plain cake. They keep well in a covered container in the refrigerator for at least a week.

SERVES 10 TO 12

- 1 cup sugar
- 1 cup sweet Marsala (see page 12)
- 1 large navel orange
- 1 cup dried apricots
- 1 cup dried peaches
- 1 cup dried figs, quartered if large
- 1 cup dried pitted prunes
- 1 cup Muscat raisins
- 2 cups water

Pour the sugar and wine into a large slow cooker. Stir well.

Remove the orange zest from the orange in long strips with a vegetable peeler. Squeeze the orange juice. Add the zest and juice to the slow cooker. Stir in the dried fruits and water.

Cover and cook on low for 2 hours, or until the fruits are tender. Let cool. Cover and refrigerate until serving time.

Apple-Raisin Cake

A simple apple cake is a welcome breakfast treat or homey dessert anytime.

SERVES 8

- 2 tablespoons plus ⅔ cup sugar
- 1 cup all-purpose flour
- 1 teaspoon baking powder
- ½ teaspoon salt
- 6 tablespoons (¾ stick) unsalted butter, softened
- 2 large eggs
- 1 teaspoon grated lemon zest
- ½ teaspoon vanilla extract
- ¼ cup milk
- 2 Golden Delicious apples (about 1 pound), cored, peeled, and chopped
- ⅓ cup dark raisins
- 2 tablespoons apricot jam

Butter and flour a 7-inch round cake pan. Sprinkle the 2 tablespoons sugar over the bottom of the pan.

Sift together the flour, baking powder, and salt.

In a large bowl with an electric mixer, beat the butter until light and fluffy. Gradually beat in the remaining ⅔ cup sugar, scraping the sides of the bowl. Beat in the eggs, one at a time, lemon zest, and vanilla until blended. On low speed, beat in half of the dry ingredients. Add the milk. Stir in the remaining dry ingredients just until smooth.

Fold in the apples and raisins. Spread the batter in the prepared pan. Place the pan in the center of a large slow cooker. Cover and cook on high for 2 hours, or until a cake tester inserted in the center comes out clean.

Transfer the pan to a rack to cool for 10 minutes. Invert the cake onto another rack and let it cool completely.

In a small saucepan or a microwave-safe bowl, heat the jam until melted. Strain the jam into a bowl. Brush the warm jam over the top of the cake. Let cool completely before serving.

Espresso-Walnut Cake

Instant espresso powder can be used to make the coffee for this cake, or if you don't want to make it yourself, buy a cup of brewed espresso at a local coffee shop. This cake is great served with a dollop of whipped cream.

SERVES 8

- ³/₄ cup unbleached all-purpose flour
- 1 tablespoon unsweetened cocoa powder
- ¹/₂ teaspoon baking powder
- ¹/₂ teaspoon ground cinnamon
- ¹/₂ teaspoon ground ginger
- ¹/₄ teaspoon salt
- 4 tablespoons (¹/₂ stick) unsalted butter, softened
- ³/₄ cup packed light brown sugar
- 2 large eggs
- 3 tablespoons cold brewed espresso
- 2 teaspoons coffee liqueur, rum, or cognac
- ¹/₂ cup chopped toasted walnuts

Butter a 7-inch springform pan or a 6-cup soufflé dish. Line the bottom of the pan with parchment paper or foil and butter the paper.

Sift together the flour, cocoa, baking powder, spices, and salt.

In a large bowl with an electric mixer, beat the butter until light and fluffy. Gradually beat in the sugar, scraping the sides of the bowl. Beat in the eggs, one at a time, until blended. Beat in the espresso and liquor. The mixture will look grainy.

With a rubber spatula, fold the dry ingredients into the butter mixture. Stir in the walnuts. Scrape the batter into the prepared pan.

Place the pan in the slow cooker. Cover and cook on high for 2 to 2½ hours, or until a toothpick inserted in the center comes out clean. Transfer to a rack to cool for 10 minutes. Invert the cake onto another rack and let it cool completely before serving.

Fig and Nut Cake

Italians don't usually bake cakes at home, probably because most live within shouting distance of a pleasant café where they can take a break and enjoy a sweet and a great cup of coffee any time of the day.

This little cake is an exception to that rule. It's the kind of thing that they like to keep on hand to enjoy when guests stop by, or even for breakfast. Dense and moist, it has sweet, chewy bits of dried figs and nuts. For a change, substitute raisins or chopped apricots for the figs.

SERVES 8

- ½ cup walnuts
- ⅔ cup dried figs (see headnote)
- ¾ cup all-purpose flour
- 1 teaspoon baking powder
- ½ teaspoon salt
- 6 tablespoons (¾ stick) unsalted butter, softened
- ½ cup sugar
- 2 large eggs
- ½ teaspoon grated lemon zest
- ¼ cup milk

Butter and flour a 7-inch round baking pan or a 6-cup baking dish.

Toast the walnuts in a large skillet over medium heat, stirring occasionally, about 5 minutes. Cool and chop. Trim off the stem ends of the figs. Chop the figs finely.

Sift together the flour, baking powder, and salt.

In a large bowl with an electric mixer, beat the butter and sugar until light and fluffy. Add the eggs, one at a time, and lemon zest and beat well. Stir in the milk. Add the dry ingredients and stir just until blended. Fold in the figs and nuts.

Scrape the batter into the prepared pan and smooth the top. Place the pan in the slow cooker. Cover and cook on high for 2 hours, or until a toothpick inserted in the center comes out clean.

Transfer the pan to a rack. Let cool for 10 minutes. Invert the cake onto another rack and let cool completely before serving.

Chocolate Truffle Cake

A deep, rich chocolate cake is the perfect dessert for any special occasion. I like to serve this one with lightly whipped cream or softened ice cream.

SERVES 6 TO 8

- 8 ounces bittersweet chocolate
- 12 tablespoons (1½ sticks) unsalted butter
- 2 tablespoons rum or strong brewed coffee
- 3 large eggs
- ½ cup sugar
- 1 teaspoon unsweetened cocoa powder

Butter a 6-cup baking dish or a 7-inch springform pan. Line the bottom of the pan with parchment paper or foil and butter the paper.

Break the chocolate into a heatproof bowl. Add the butter. Place the bowl over a pan of simmering water. The water should not touch the bottom of the bowl. When the chocolate is softened, remove the bowl from the heat and stir until blended and smooth. Stir in the rum or coffee.

In a medium bowl, beat the eggs with the sugar until light and pale yellow. Stir the egg mixture into the chocolate. Scrape the batter into the prepared pan.

Place the pan in the slow cooker. Cover and cook on high for 2 hours, or until set.

Remove the pan from the slow cooker. Cover and chill for several hours or overnight. To serve, run a small knife around the edge of the cake. Invert it onto a serving plate. Place the cocoa powder in a small strainer and sprinkle it over the cake.

Polenta-Pear Cake

This simple cake has a golden color from the cornmeal and a dense texture. It is very satisfying with a cup of tea.

SERVES 6 TO 8

2 tablespoons plus ¾ cup sugar

1 large ripe pear, cored and thinly sliced

1 cup all-purpose flour

¼ cup finely ground yellow cornmeal

1½ teaspoons baking powder

1 teaspoon salt

12 tablespoons (1½ sticks) unsalted butter, softened

2 large eggs

½ teaspoon grated lemon zest

½ cup milk

Butter and flour a 7-inch round cake pan. Sprinkle the 2 tablespoons sugar over the bottom of the pan. Arrange the pear slices in the pan in a pinwheel fashion, overlapping them slightly.

Sift together the flour, cornmeal, baking powder, and salt.

In a large bowl with an electric mixer, beat the butter until light and fluffy. Gradually beat in the remaining ¾ cup sugar, scraping the sides of the bowl. Beat in the eggs, one at a time, and lemon zest until blended. On low speed, beat in half of the dry ingredients. Add the milk. Stir in the remaining dry ingredients just until smooth. Scrape the batter into the prepared pan, spreading it evenly over the pears. Place the pan in the slow cooker.

Cover and cook on high for 3 hours, or until a toothpick inserted in the center comes out clean. Cool on a rack for 10 minutes. Invert the cake onto another rack and let it cool completely before serving.

Pumpkin Cake with Tipsy Raisins

This is a great cake for fall and winter meals and snacking. The pumpkin adds a beautiful sunny color and moisture without making it heavy, and the spices and brandy- or grappa-soaked raisins give it a warm and appealing flavor. Apple or orange juice can be used in place of the brandy, if you prefer.

SERVES 8

- ½ cup golden raisins
- ¼ cup brandy, grappa, or rum (see headnote)
- 1½ cups all-purpose flour
- 1 teaspoon baking powder
- 1 teaspoon baking soda
- ½ teaspoon salt
- ½ teaspoon ground cinnamon
- ½ teaspoon ground nutmeg
- ½ cup sugar
- ½ cup packed dark brown sugar
- ⅓ cup canola oil
- 2 large eggs, beaten
- 1 cup fresh or canned pumpkin or other cooked winter squash puree
- ½ cup chopped toasted walnuts

In a small bowl, combine the raisins and brandy, grappa, or rum. Let stand for 30 minutes.

Butter and flour a 7-inch springform pan or a 6-cup baking pan.

Sift the flour, baking powder, baking soda, salt, cinnamon, and nutmeg onto a piece of wax paper.

In a large bowl, beat the sugars and oil. Add the eggs and pumpkin and mix well. Add the dry ingredients. Add the nuts and raisins with the soaking liquid.

Pour the batter into the prepared pan. Place several paper towels on top of the pan to absorb excess moisture. Cover and cook on high for 2 to 2½ hours, or until a toothpick inserted in the center of the cake comes out clean.

Transfer the pan to a rack and let cool for 10 minutes. Invert the cake onto another rack and let cool completely before serving.

Ricotta Amaretti Cheesecake with Blueberry Sauce

Crunchy Italian almond cookies called *amaretti* are widely available in supermarkets, but you can substitute vanilla wafers or other cookie crumbs in the crust.

If you don't have a rack for your slow cooker, make a ring out of crumpled foil and place it in the insert to prevent the cake pan from coming into direct contact with the hot surface. You can save the ring and reuse it.

SERVES 8

CRUST

²/₃ cup amaretti cookie crumbs (about 30 cookies)

3 tablespoons melted unsalted butter

1 tablespoon sugar

FILLING

1 15-ounce container (2 cups) whole-milk ricotta cheese

8 ounces cream cheese, softened

²/₃ cup sugar

3 large eggs

1 teaspoon grated lemon zest

1 teaspoon grated orange zest

1 tablespoon fresh lemon juice

1 teaspoon vanilla extract

SAUCE

2 cups blueberries, fresh or frozen

2 tablespoons sugar

3 tablespoons water

1 teaspoon cornstarch

Butter a 7-inch springform pan. Tear off a large square of aluminum foil and place the pan in the center of the foil. Fold the foil up the sides of the pan so that water cannot enter. Place a small rack in the center of a large slow cooker (see headnote).

MAKE THE CRUST: In a small bowl, stir together the cookie crumbs, butter, and sugar. Press mixture firmly into the base of the pan. Place the pan in the refrigerator.

MAKE THE FILLING: In a food processor or with an electric mixer, beat together the ricotta, cream cheese, and sugar until smooth.

Add the eggs, one at a time, blending until incorporated. Add the lemon and orange zest, lemon juice, and vanilla extract and blend until smooth. Scrape the mixture into the prepared crust.

Place the pan on the rack in the slow cooker. Pour 1 cup hot water into the cooker. Cover and cook on high for 2 hours, or until the cheesecake is set around the edge but slightly soft and jiggly in the center. Remove the lid, turn off the cooker, and allow the cheesecake to stand in the cooker until the pan is cool enough to handle. Transfer the pan to a rack, cool to room temperature, then cover and refrigerate for several hours or overnight.

MAKE THE SAUCE: Combine the berries, sugar, and 2 tablespoons of the water in a small saucepan. Bring the mixture to a simmer over medium heat. Stir until the sugar is dissolved. In a small cup, stir together the cornstarch and the remaining 1 tablespoon water. Pour the cornstarch mixture into the center of the simmering sauce and stir until thickened, about 1 minute. Pour into a covered container and refrigerate.

To serve, run a knife around the inside of the cake pan. Remove the ring. Slice the cake and drizzle with sauce.

Goat Cheese Cheesecake
with Orange-Fig Sauce

Made fresh daily from sheep's milk, the ricotta in Sicily has a tangy flavor and creamy texture that is quite unlike the cow's-milk ricotta common in this country. To try to duplicate that flavor, I combined ricotta with goat cheese and came up with this delightful cake. I like to serve it with dried figs poached in orange juice, but fresh raspberries or strawberries are good too.

SERVES 8

CRUST

- ⅔ cup vanilla wafer crumbs (about 16 wafers)
- 3 tablespoons melted unsalted butter
- 1 tablespoon sugar

FILLING

- 1 15-ounce container (2 cups) whole-milk ricotta cheese
- 6 ounces fresh goat cheese, cut up
- ¼ cup heavy cream
- ¾ cup sugar
- 2 large eggs
- ½ teaspoon grated lemon zest
- 1 tablespoon fresh lemon juice
- 1 teaspoon vanilla extract

SAUCE

- ¾ cup orange juice
- 2 tablespoons honey
- 1 7- to 8-ounce package dried Calimyrna figs (see headnote), stemmed and cut into quarters
- 1 3-inch strip orange zest

Butter a 7-inch springform pan. Tear off a large square of aluminum foil and place the pan in the center of the foil. Fold the foil up the sides of the pan so that water cannot enter. Place a small rack in the center of a large slow cooker (see headnote on page 217).

MAKE THE CRUST: In a small bowl, stir together the wafer crumbs, butter, and sugar. Scatter the mixture in the prepared pan, pressing it firmly into the base of the pan. Place the pan in the refrigerator while you prepare the filling.

MAKE THE FILLING: In a food processor or with an electric mixer, combine all the ingredients. Process until smooth and creamy. Scrape the mixture into the prepared crust. Place the pan on the rack in the slow cooker. Pour 1 cup hot water into the cooker.

Cover and cook on high for 2½ hours, or until the cake is set around the edges but still slightly soft and jiggly in the center. Remove the lid and turn off the cooker. Allow the cheesecake to stand in the cooker until the pan is cool enough to handle. Transfer the pan to a rack, cool to room temperature, then cover and refrigerate for several hours or overnight.

MAKE THE SAUCE: Combine the orange juice and honey in a small saucepan. Bring it to a simmer over medium heat. Add the figs and orange zest. Cook until the figs are soft and tender, about 10 minutes. Let cool. Refrigerate in a covered container until ready to serve.

To serve, run a knife around the inside of the cake pan. Remove the ring. Slice the cake and top with a spoonful of the fig sauce.

Panettone Bread Pudding

Every year at Christmastime, I look forward to eating panettone, a traditional sweet bread from Milan. We enjoy it with a glass of spumante for an elegant dessert or toasted and spread with mascarpone for holiday brunch.

If you like, add half a cup of raisins or other chopped dried fruit to the pudding. And you can substitute brioche, challah, or good-quality white bread for the panettone.

SERVES 8

- 3 large eggs
- ¾ cup sugar
- 2 cups milk
- 1 cup heavy cream
- ¼ cup Marsala (see page 12) or sherry
- 2 teaspoons grated orange zest
- ½ teaspoon ground cinnamon
- 6 ounces panettone (see headnote), cut into 1-inch cubes
- Ice cream or whipped heavy cream for serving

Butter the insert of a large slow cooker.

In a large bowl with an electric mixer, beat the eggs and sugar until pale and foamy. Beat in the milk, cream, wine, orange zest, and cinnamon.

Stir in the bread cubes and pour the mixture into the slow cooker. Cover and cook on high for 4 hours, or until the center is set and a knife inserted in the center comes out clean. Serve warm or chilled, either plain or with ice cream or whipped cream.

Index

Page references in *italic* refer to illustrations